My Name *is* Not

*Refusing Every Name
Pain Tried To Give Me*

by

DAFFNIE MANSELL

Publisher: Corey A. Marchand Publishing Enterprises, LLC

Contact: Cam.publishingllc@gmail.com

ISBN: 979-8-90417-781-2

ABOUT THE AUTHOR

Daffnie Mansell is a woman of faith, resilience, and transformation whose life reflects the redemptive power of God's grace. She is passionate about helping others break free from the labels, wounds, and limitations of their past and guiding them toward a renewed understanding of their true identity in God. Her life and message testify that healing is possible, purpose is intentional, and no one is beyond restoration.

Through life's many challenges, Daffnie has learned that healing requires honesty, surrender, and courage. She understands the necessity of releasing what no longer serves the future God has ordained and embracing the beauty of becoming who He always intended. Her journey has been shaped by perseverance and marked by an unwavering trust in God, even in seasons of loss, uncertainty, and deep personal growth. Each step has strengthened her resolve to live authentically and walk boldly in obedience.

Daffnie carries a genuine heart for people and a voice that speaks life, truth, and restoration. Whether through prayer, encouragement, or teaching, she creates safe and sacred spaces where healing can begin, faith can grow, and transformation can take root. Her ministry is grounded in compassion and fueled by the belief that

every individual deserves to experience freedom,
wholeness, and hope.

My Name Is Not is her personal declaration and
prophetic reminder that pain does not define purpose and
past experiences do not have the authority to rename
what God has already called whole. It is a bold statement
of freedom, identity, and truth that invites others to
confront shame, reject false labels, and embrace the
name God has spoken over their lives.

Daffnie continues to walk in purpose, inspiring others to
release what they have carried for too long, reclaim their
God-given identity, and step confidently into who they
were created to be. Through her life, her faith, and her
voice, she serves as a living testimony that
transformation is possible and that God's grace always
has the final word.

A NOTE FROM THE AUTHOR

If you have find yourself within these pages, I want you to pause and receive this truth with an open heart. You are not too damaged. You are not behind some invisible line where hope no longer reaches. You are not finished, forgotten, or beyond repair.

Healing does not always announce itself with noise or certainty. Often it arrives gently, almost unnoticed. It unfolds in a single honest prayer whispered through trembling lips. It takes shape in one boundary that finally honors your worth. It lives in one tear that you no longer force back, one breath where your chest loosens at last, one sacred moment when you stop shrinking to survive and begin returning to who you truly are.

Where shame once told you to lower your head and stay small, God is the lifter of your head, steady and kind. Where trauma tried to rename you with fear, loss, or silence, God calls you Beloved and speaks it with intention. Where the past attempted to trap you in old rooms of pain, God speaks forward, opening doors you never thought would move.

Your name is not what happened to you when you had no control. Your name is not what you endured to make it through another day. Your name is not what you lost, nor what was taken from you.

Your name is held in Him, spoken with purpose, covered in grace, and carried with unfailing love.

With love, faith, and truth,
Daffnie I. Mansell

DEDICATION

To every woman who is learning how to breathe again after holding her pain for far too long. This is for you.

To the woman who carries quiet wars behind a practiced smile, who pours love into everyone else while slowly trying to remember who she was before the hurting began. To the one who stays strong out loud but feels tired in the silence. I see you.

This book is dedicated to the women who have endured trauma, heartbreak, rejection, and seasons that tried to rewrite their worth. To the women who were wounded in places no one noticed and were expected to heal without guidance, supported only by their own will to survive. To the ones who kept going even when the weight felt unbearable and when the pain felt defining.

Let this be your reminder:

You are not what happened to you.
You are not the abuse that tried to erase your voice.
You are not the betrayal that broke your trust.
You are not the abandonment that made you question your value.
You are not the pain that attempted to name you or claim you as its own.

You are still worthy of love that is gentle and safe.
You are still valuable, beyond what was taken or lost.

You are still whole, even if you are healing in fragments and rediscovering yourself piece by piece.

May these words meet you where you are and wrap around you like grace.
May they remind you that your story did not end in your brokenness and that your future is not confined by your past.
May you find the courage to release every label trauma tried to place on you and boldly walk in the truth of who you are becoming.

This is for the woman who is rising, even when it hurts. The woman who chooses healing again and again, one breath, one step, and one day at a time.

You are not what happened to you.

Daffnie I. Mansell

ACKNOWLEDGEMENTS

First and foremost, I give all honor and glory to my Lord and Savior, Jesus Christ, from whom every good and perfect gift flows. I thank Him for sparing my life, for keeping and covering me when I could not cover myself, and for giving me the strength to endure. In moments of weakness, He was my strong tower. In moments of uncertainty, He was my clarity. This journey exists only because of His grace, His mercy, and His sustaining power that allowed me to rise, recover, and remain resilient.

To my niece, Deneisha Marchand,

Thank you for your time, your patience, and your willingness to truly listen. Allowing you into the heart of this work, chapter by chapter, was a gift I do not take lightly. Your honest feedback, thoughtful insights, and authentic reactions helped shape this book in ways that mattered most.

Your voice and perspective brought clarity where I needed refinement and affirmation where I needed courage. Every conversation we shared reminded me that this work was not being created in isolation. Thank you for your love, your support, and your truth. This book is stronger because of you, and I am incredibly grateful.

To Rasheedah Ahmad,

I want to sincerely thank you for your unwavering prayers and constant encouragement throughout this journey. In moments when the weight felt heavy and my energy began to fade, your words lifted me. When my strength ran low, your prayers carried me.

You reminded me, sometimes gently and sometimes boldly, that God was present in every step, even when I struggled to recognize it myself. Thank you for believing in me, for speaking life into me, and for covering me when I did not even have the words to pray. Your support has been a sacred gift, and I hold deep gratitude for you.

To Will Armstead,

Thank you for believing in me, especially during moments when my own belief wavered. Your encouragement, confidence, and steady presence served as a constant reminder of my ability to see this through.

You had a way of affirming my strength and purpose even when I questioned my capacity to finish. Your belief fueled this vision and helped keep it moving forward. I am truly thankful for your support and for the role you played in this journey.

To my sisters, The Elite 8: Tanesha Jones, Jalene Henley, Allurah Rezendes-Williams, Jacqueline

Gonzalez, Tracy Brown, Cynthia Sanchez, Jacquie Martinez, and our fearless leader, Kaitlyn Swoope,

Thank you for being my safe place, my refuge in every season. You have been my comfort zone, my laughter on hard days, and my strength in silent moments when words fell short.

Your love, loyalty, and unwavering support have carried me more than you may ever know. Thank you for seeing the God-given potential in me when I struggled to see it myself, and for never allowing me to forget who I am. I love you all deeply, to life.

Last, but certainly not least, to My Pastor and Dear Friend, Dr. Michael J. Hill,

Thank you for pushing me beyond my comfort zones and challenging me to grow in ways I did not always choose, but desperately needed. Thank you for covering me in prayer and for standing with me through moments that demanded faith, resilience, and perseverance.

I am especially grateful for the difficult conversations, the ones that stretched me, sharpened me, and shaped me. Your guidance, honesty, and steadfast support have left an indelible mark on my life and on this journey. Thank you for walking with me as I continue becoming who God has called me to be.

TABLE OF CONTENTS

Chapter One: What I Carried That Was Never Mine

Chapter Two: When Letting Go Felt Unsafe

Chapter Three: The Names I Answered To

Chapter Four: Breaking Agreement With Shame

Chapter Five: The Weight of Unshed Tears

Chapter Six: The Weight of Memory

Chapter Seven: Beyond What Me

Chapter Eight: The Wall That Pain Built

Chapter Nine: Unveiling your True Potential

Chapter Ten: Triggers and Traumas

Chapter Eleven: The Reintroduction

INTRODUCTION

This book begins as a testimony, not of perfection, not of arrival, but of transformation. It is written from the sacred intersection where faith meets truth, where pain is no longer hidden or minimized, yet is no longer permitted to dictate the future. *My Name Is Not* is a declaration that identity is restored by God alone, not determined by circumstance, not shaped by loss, and not confined by the chapters that came before.

There comes a moment when mere survival no longer satisfies the soul. A moment when endurance feels hollow, when breathing is not the same as living, and when the heart can no longer carry its wounds in silence. In that moment, faith does not ask for comfort. It calls for courage. Courage to speak, to remember, to believe again, and to give voice to what has long gone unspoken.

This book was born in that moment.

It rises from seasons where silence felt safer than truth, where concealment seemed wiser than honesty. It was shaped in days when starting over felt far heavier than staying broken, when familiar pain felt less terrifying than unknown hope. Yet even there, even then, grace continued to call, persistent and patient, and faith, though weary, kept answering.

Scripture promises that God is close to the brokenhearted and rescues those who are crushed in spirit. That truth did not erase the struggle, nor did it bypass the grief. Instead, it reframed everything. What was meant to destroy became the soil where resilience took root. What once felt like disqualification revealed itself as preparation. The places that bore the deepest ache became the very ground where healing began to speak.

"Behold, I am doing a new thing; now it springs forth, do you not perceive it?" Isaiah 43:19

This book is written for the version of me who once wondered, quietly and desperately, if renewal was still possible. It is written for anyone who has worn labels handed to them by trauma, failure, rejection, abandonment, or loss, and over time began to believe those labels were permanent. Faith revealed something truer and far more powerful. Names spoken by pain are temporary, but names spoken by God are eternal.

In Christ, identity is not earned, repaired, or negotiated. It is received. The past may explain the wound, but it does not determine the worth. Scripture declares that those who are in Christ are made new, not revised, not improved, not patched together, but reborn. That revelation became the foundation for every page that follows.

This is not a story about forgetting what happened. It is a
testimony of refusing to allow what happened to rule
what is becoming. Faith does not deny reality. It declares
authority over it. It acknowledges the scar while
proclaiming the healing. It tells the truth about the pain
while refusing to surrender the future to it.

A Declaration of Faith

My Name Is Not is a refusal to answer to shame, fear, or
condemnation. It is a faith-filled acknowledgment that
God's voice carries greater weight than history, than
memory, than any verdict spoken in moments of
brokenness. Where the past attempted to pronounce
finality, God spoke purpose. Where weakness was
exposed, strength was supplied. This book stands as
evidence that God restores identity before He changes
circumstances.

It testifies that healing is not only possible. It is
promised. That beginning again is not failure when God
is the author. That redemption often unfolds quietly,
faithfully, and with holy persistence long before it is ever
visible.

As you turn these pages, may you recognize the places
where faith sustained you, even when you did not realize
it was holding you upright. May you see how grace was
working in the shadows, how God was present in the
pauses, the waiting, and even the unanswered questions.

And may you be reminded that your story is not finished,
that your life is still being written, and that your true
name, your eternal name, is held securely in Him.

<u>Opening Declaration</u>

I am not what I endured.
I am not what I lost.
I am not what broke me.
I am not the name pain tried to give me.

I belong to God.
I am becoming whole.
I am learning to trust again.
And my story, by His grace, is still being written.

Chapter One

What I Carried That Was Never Mine

Key Scriptures

"Come to Me, all who are weary and burdened, and I
will give you rest."
(Matthew 11:28)

"Cast all your cares on Him, because He cares for you."
(1 Peter 5:7)

"You did not receive a spirit of slavery to fall back into
fear, but you received the Spirit of adoption."
(Romans 8:15)

What This Chapter Holds

Some burdens arrive so early and stay so long that they
stop feeling like weight and start feeling like identity.

Some responsibility was never assigned to you.
Some guilt never belonged in your hands.
Some blame found you not because you were guilty, but
because you were present.

This chapter is the first act of separation.
What happened around me is not the same as what
belongs to me.

And God does not require me to carry what He never assigned.

This is where the story truly begins, not with events, but with burdens. With the invisible loads we learned to carry in order to survive. With the quiet reckoning that comes when faith reveals what was never meant to be held.

The Chapter

I learned how to carry things long before I learned how to name them.

Before language, there was weight.
Before understanding, there was responsibility.
Before choice, there was endurance.

I carried rejection before I knew what it was called. I carried betrayal without having the words to describe it. I carried guilt that formed in the absence of explanation, and blame that settled into my body simply because I was nearby. I carried silence, the kind that teaches you not to ask questions, not to need, and not to speak unless spoken to.

No one placed these burdens in my hands and said, "This is yours."
They came quietly. Slowly. Invisibly.
They arrived so early that I assumed they were part of me.

I carried emotions too heavy for a child. I carried responsibility without authority, awareness without protection, and expectations without permission. I learned how to manage other people's moods, anticipate disappointment, and adjust myself accordingly. Somewhere in all that carrying, I forgot what it felt like to stand upright without bracing for impact.

At some point, endurance became my identity. Strength became synonymous with silence.

I believed that if I could hold everything together, nothing would fall apart. If I absorbed enough pain, tension, and disappointment, maybe no one else would have to. I measured my worth by how much I could endure without breaking. Pain became familiar. Carrying became instinctive. Letting go felt reckless, even dangerous, as if release would undo everything I had worked so hard to keep intact.

I carried what other people refused to face.
I carried the emotional debris of choices I did not make.
I carried the consequences of dysfunction I did not create.

I carried shame without ever being told I should, which somehow made it heavier. When things went wrong, I searched myself for the fault. When someone hurt me, I assumed I must have deserved it. When rooms filled with tension and silence, I learned how to disappear inside myself to keep the peace.

There is a particular kind of loneliness that comes from carrying what was never yours.

It separates you from rest.
It convinces you that love must be earned.
It whispers that laying anything down would be selfish, lazy, or ungrateful.

So I kept carrying.

I carried through seasons that demanded more than I had. I carried into relationships that mistook my endurance for permission. I carried into faith, assuming God expected from me the same relentless strength I demanded of myself. I thought obedience meant heaviness. I thought faith required exhaustion.

But God does not ask us to carry what He never assigned.

That truth did not arrive dramatically. It came gently and almost reluctantly through moments when my strength failed and grace met me anyway. It came through prayers stripped of performance. Through tears I did not know how to explain. Through the realization that I was tired not because I lacked faith, but because I had been holding burdens God never placed in my hands.

I began to recognize how early I had learned to substitute control for safety. Carrying made me feel prepared and alert. If I stayed strong and vigilant, maybe nothing could surprise me again.

But faith is not built on control.
Faith is built on trust.
Trust requires release.

There was grief in that realization. Grief for years spent striving. Grief for the version of me who believed love was conditional. Grief for the times I blamed myself for things that were not my fault. Healing did not erase those memories, but it gave them meaning. It showed me that survival taught me habits faith would one day need to undo.

I carried responsibility for other people's emotions.
I carried the need to be agreeable, dependable, and unproblematic.
I carried the belief that usefulness was the same as value.

I carried fear disguised as wisdom and silence disguised as peace. I carried strength learned in places that were never safe. Because I carried these things for so long, laying them down felt like betrayal, as if I were abandoning a role I had been given without consent.

God's invitation was never harsh. It was patient. It sounded less like correction and more like permission.

Permission to rest.
Permission to be human.
Permission to admit that I was tired.

Faith did not shame me for carrying too much. It gently asked why I believed I had to.

There is a sacred unlearning that happens when God restores identity. He does not only add truth. He removes lies. He reveals the difference between what shaped you and what defines you. Some of what I called maturity was actually self-protection. Some of what I called strength was learned in unsafe places. Some of what I called faith was survival dressed in spiritual language.

Letting go was not one moment. It was many small surrenders.

Surrendering the need to explain myself.
Surrendering the weight of outcomes I could not control.
Surrendering the belief that I owed everyone access to me.

Each release felt unfamiliar, but lighter. For the first time, obedience did not feel like carrying more. It felt like carrying less.

I began to understand that Jesus never invited people to add burdens to their lives. He invited them to lay burdens down. He never glorified exhaustion. He never equated suffering with worth. Rest was not a reward for faithfulness. It was His response to weariness.

What I carried shaped my posture. It bent me inward. It trained me to brace for impact instead of expect provision. Faith slowly straightened what fear had curved. It taught me that trust does not ignore pain, but it also refuses to let pain be the final authority.

This chapter is not about blame. It is about clarity. It is about distinguishing responsibility from false ownership, compassion from self erasure, endurance from calling. Naming what was never mine was the first step toward reclaiming what always was: my voice, my rest, and my identity.

I did not lose strength when I laid those burdens down. I found it. Strength rooted in truth instead of fear. Strength rooted in grace instead of striving.

God was never waiting for me to prove my capacity. He was waiting for me to trust His.

What I carried once kept me alive. It was not meant to lead my life.

When I finally laid it down, there was room for freedom that does not require explanation, faith that does not demand exhaustion, and an identity no longer defined by what I survived, but by who God says I am.

This was the beginning.
Not of forgetting, but of release.
Not of denial, but of truth.

The moment I realized what I carried was never mine,
was the moment I finally learned how to walk
unburdened.

REFLECTION

Name It. Release It. Replace It.

This moment is an invitation, not an obligation. You are not being asked to uncover everything at once, only to begin noticing what you have been holding. Some burdens were picked up so early that you never questioned them. Others were carried so faithfully they felt sacred. This reflection gently separates what shaped you from what belongs to you now.

Name it:

What burdens did I pick up so early that they slowly became part of how I see myself? What responsibilities, emotions, or expectations did I absorb before I had the language or power to decline them?

Release it:

What am I still carrying today that God never placed in my hands? What feels heavy not because it is holy, but because it was never meant to be mine?

Replace it:

What truth is God offering me now in place of the lie that convinced me I had to carry this to be loved, accepted, or safe?

Reflection sentence:

God does not ask me to carry what He never assigned.

Journaling Prompts

1. The first responsibility I took on that was never mine was born in the moment when I needed safety, approval, or peace, and it taught me that carrying was how I survived.

2. The burden I keep revisiting out of fear is the one I believe protects me, even though it exhausts me. I return to it because letting go feels uncertain.

3. The lie that made me useful but depleted was the belief that my value depended on how much I could hold, fix, or endure without complaint.

4. If I stopped carrying this, I fear that something would fall apart, someone would be disappointed, or I would finally be seen as insufficient.

5. The kindest permission God is giving me right now is an invitation to stop striving, stop proving, and stop surviving situations that no longer exist.

PRAYER

Father, in the name of Jesus, I come before You with open hands and an honest heart. I lay down what was never mine to carry. You did not call me Your own because of my endurance, my strength, or what I survived. You called me because You are faithful and You chose me. Your Word declares that I did not receive a spirit of slavery to return to fear, but the Spirit of adoption by which I am called Your child. Today, I choose to stop living as though survival defines me.

You say that I am chosen, set apart, and known by You. You call me a chosen generation, a royal priesthood, a holy nation, and Your own special possession. Help me release every false responsibility I accepted just to feel safe. Help me loosen my grip on misplaced guilt, borrowed shame, and expectations rooted in fear rather than trust. Where I learned to strive, teach me to trust. Where I learned to carry alone, teach me to rest in You.

Search my heart gently and reveal what does not belong there. You promise that I can cast every care on You because You care for me. I give You the weight of unspoken expectations, the need to control outcomes, and the belief that love must be earned through endurance. Replace these with truth that steadies me, peace that guards me, and confidence rooted in You rather than performance.

Align my thoughts with what You have already declared to be true. You promise to keep in perfect peace those whose minds are stayed on You. Straighten what fear has bent within me. Heal what silence has hidden. Restore what striving has exhausted. Teach me to walk forward guided by purpose, not pressured by fear.

I receive the rest You promised. You invited the weary and burdened to come to You, and You promised rest without condition. I step forward now unburdened, no longer defined by what I carried, but by who You say I am. I surrender not because I am weak, but because I trust You.

I walk in freedom, clarity, and quiet confidence, knowing You are leading me. I am Yours, and I am enough. Amen.

CHAPTER ONE CLOSING DECLARATION

I release false ownership and the belief that everything depends on me.
I release borrowed responsibility and the pressure to carry what is not mine.
I release the lie that love must be proven through exhaustion.

I accept God's rest as obedience.
I accept God's truth as my identity.
I accept God's covering as sufficient and complete.

What I carried helped me survive, but it will not
determine how I live.

Chapter Two

When Letting Go Felt Unsafe

Key Scriptures

"Cast your burden on the Lord, and He will sustain you."
Psalm 55:22

"You will keep in perfect peace those whose minds are
stayed on You."
Isaiah 26:3

"Trust in the Lord with all your heart and lean not on
your own understanding."
Proverbs 3:5

"God is our refuge and strength, a very present help in
trouble."
Psalm 46:1

What This Chapter Holds

Letting go sounds like freedom, until you actually do it.

Because sometimes the weight you carried was not only
a burden. It was a framework. A brace. A way of
standing upright in a world that never stopped asking.

The weight gave your days shape.
It kept you occupied enough not to feel what hurt.
Needed enough to feel secure.
Alert enough to believe you could prevent the next loss.

So when you finally released it, you did not just lose pressure. You lost familiarity.

This chapter is about the withdrawal symptoms of healing. The ache that comes when noise disappears, the fear that emerges when your hands are suddenly empty, the vulnerability of discovering how exposed trust can feel.

Letting go did not feel unsafe because God was absent. Letting go felt unsafe because the survival system that once protected you was no longer allowed to lead.

Interlude: Control Can Feel Like Covering

There is a difference between being covered and being in control.

Control whispers, "If I manage it carefully enough, I can survive it."

Covering says, "Even if I lose my grip, God will still hold me."

Control feels safer because it keeps your hands busy. Covering feels dangerous because it requires trust.

And trust is hard when you have been disappointed, abandoned, or hurt.

So, if your hands tremble while you surrender, that does not mean you are weak. Something old is loosening.

It means healing has begun.

I thought laying it down would feel like immediate relief. I imagined peace arriving all at once, like finally exhaling after years of holding my breath. I believed I would feel lighter, steadier, and grateful.

Instead, I felt exposed.

The weight was gone, but so was the structure it had given my life. Carrying had become my way of staying upright. It told me where to stand and what to do. Without it, I had no clear place to put my hands, no familiar tension to lean against. The silence felt louder than the noise ever had.

Letting go felt unsafe because carrying had become familiar. It had given me a role, someone reliable, someone strong, someone always ready. It offered usefulness in exchange for exhaustion. When I released what was never mine to hold, I also released the illusion of control that came with it. I lost my script. I no longer knew how to anticipate every outcome or brace for impact. Faith asked me to stand without armor, and that felt like stepping into the open with nothing to shield my chest.

There is a grief that comes with healing, a quiet, confusing grief. Not grief for the pain itself, but for the coping mechanisms that once kept you alive. I mourned the certainty of being needed. I missed knowing exactly how to respond, even when the cost was my peace. I missed the identity that carrying had given me, even though it was built on constant depletion. Letting go created space, and space can feel like loss long before it feels like freedom.

I began to realize how much of my life had been shaped by reaction. I was always responding, adjusting to someone else's needs, someone else's moods, someone else's emergencies. Without those demands filling my time, I was left with myself. Stillness confronted me. Silence exposed what busyness had buried. Rest felt undeserved, almost irresponsible. I had to learn that safety does not always come from preparedness. Sometimes it comes from trust.

Fear was persistent. It told me that letting go meant being careless. That stepping back meant failure. That if something fell apart, it would be because I had stopped holding it together. The fear sounded reasonable, almost wise, but it was rooted in control. Faith does not deny risk. It reframes responsibility. It reminds us that outcomes were never meant to rest entirely on our shoulders.

There were moments I wanted to pick the burden back up, not because it was healthy, but because it was known. Carrying had given me purpose, even if it was borrowed and heavy. Letting go forced me to sit with uncertainty, to resist filling the silence with old habits. I learned that trust is not passive. It is an active decision to remain open when fear insists on retreat.

Obedience began to look different. Before, it was driven by urgency, by proving my devotion through endurance. Now, obedience asked for presence. It required listening instead of rushing, responding instead of anticipating. God was teaching me that faith is not measured by how much I can withstand, but by how willing I am to rely on Him.

Vulnerability became unavoidable. Without the burden to hide behind, my weaknesses were visible, especially to myself. I could no longer confuse busyness with strength or silence with maturity. I had to face the parts of me that were tired, uncertain, and still healing. And there, in that exposure, I encountered a grace that did not require performance.

Letting go reshaped my relationships as well. Some people struggled with the boundaries I set. Others did not know how to engage with me without the version of me who carried everything. The loss was painful, but it was also clarifying. It revealed which connections were sustained by mutual presence and which were sustained by my exhaustion. Trusting God sometimes means allowing distance where dependence once existed.

There were days when peace felt fragile. Days when rest felt like neglect. Days when surrender felt like a mistake. But even then, something was shifting. I was no longer collapsing under the weight. I was learning to stand. Unsteady, trembling, but upright. Faith became less about certainty and more about consent, a willingness to be led.

God did not hurry me through this process. He did not shame my hesitation or demand instant confidence. He remained present in the discomfort, gently reminding me that safety is not found in control, but in Him. I did not have to understand every step to take the next one.

Over time, the space created by letting go began to change. What once felt like exposure slowly became room to breathe. Silence softened. Rest no longer felt threatening. I learned the difference between being unguarded and being unprotected. God was not asking me to be reckless. He was inviting me to be covered by Him, not by my own effort.

When letting go felt unsafe, it revealed how deeply I had equated control with care. I believed that if I stopped holding everything together, everything would fall apart. What actually fell away was the lie that I was the glue.

God did not need my exhaustion to sustain what He had already ordained.

This chapter is about the courage to remain surrendered when surrender feels uncomfortable. It is about resisting the urge to reclaim what God has asked you to release. It is about trusting that the unfamiliar can still be holy.

Letting go did not make me reckless.
It made me reliant.

And in that reliance, I discovered a deeper, quieter strength.

I am still learning that safety is not the absence of uncertainty, but the presence of God. When letting go felt unsafe, faith taught me to stay anyway. That choice, made again and again, became the bridge between surviving and trusting, between carrying and being carried.

This was not the end of the struggle.
But it was the end of facing it alone.

And that made all the difference.

REFLECTION

Name It, Release It, Replace It

Name it:
What did carrying this give me, beyond the weight
itself?
It gave me something to lean on when faith felt risky.
It offered structure when life felt unpredictable.
It gave me an identity I could explain and a purpose I
could defend,
a sense of belonging built on usefulness,
a kind of control that felt like protection, even when it
cost me peace.

Release it:
What am I tempted to pick back up, not because it
belongs to me,
but because it is familiar?
What do my hands reach for when silence feels unsafe,
when ease feels undeserved,
when resting feels like abandoning responsibility?
What have I mistaken for stewardship
when it was really fear in disguise?

Replace it:
What does God want to give me in the empty space?
Not absence, but invitation.
Rest that does not require earning.
Covering that does not depend on my effort.

Boundaries that keep me whole instead of needed.
A confidence rooted in who He is, not what I carry.
Peace that stays even when answers do not come
quickly.

Truth to repeat:
I am not uncovered.
I am being covered differently.

JOURNALING PROMPTS

1. When I first let go, I felt __________ because
    __________.
    What surfaced immediately, relief, fear, grief, or
    disorientation?

2. The "illusion of control" looked like __________
    in my life.
    Where did I confuse vigilance with wisdom?

3. The space God created is forcing me to face
    __________.
    What can no longer be avoided now that the
    noise is gone?

4. The relationship or relationships shifting because
    of my boundaries are __________.
    What feels painful? What feels clarifying?

5. The new kind of obedience God is teaching me is
    ___________.

    How is faith being practiced differently now?

6. If I trusted God fully here, I would ___________.
    What would I stop bracing for?

AFFIRMATION

I release what once felt necessary,
even when letting go feels unfamiliar and vulnerable.

I am safe, even without the weight I used to carry.
I do not need control to be covered.
I do not need pressure to have purpose.
I do not need exhaustion to prove my worth.

I trust God in the space where certainty used to live.
I trust Him when my hands are empty
and my heart is learning new rhythms.

I allow myself to stand without bracing for impact.
I allow rest without guilt.
I allow faith to replace fear, one step at a time.

I am not exposed. I am held.
I am not careless. I am covered.
I am not falling behind. I am being led.

What once kept me alive no longer defines me.
I honor the survival, and I choose the healing.

I do not rush this process.
I do not retreat into old habits.
I remain present in the unfolding.

God goes before me, walks beside me, and stays with
me.
I am learning that safety is found in His presence,
not in my control.

I let go, even when my voice shakes.
I trust, even when the path feels quiet.
I stand, even when my strength feels new.

I am carried now.
And I am safe.

BREATH PRAYER

(This page is meant to be slow. Read it out loud.)

Inhale: God, You are my refuge.
Exhale: I release control.

Inhale: You go before me.
Exhale: I do not have to brace.

Inhale: You are present help.
Exhale: I am not alone.

Inhale: Your peace guards me.
Exhale: I am safe.

CHAPTER TWO CLOSING DECLARATION

I will not return to what God delivered me from.
I will not pick up what He gently and clearly asked me to release.
I will not confuse familiarity with safety.

Empty hands are not weakness.
They are evidence of surrender,
proof that I am trusting someone stronger than myself.

I am not uncovered.
I am not unsafe.
I am learning trust.

And God is teaching me
how to live,
unburdened.

Chapter Three

The Names I Answered To

KEY SCRIPTURES

"See what great love the Father has lavished on us, that we should be called children of God. And that is what we are."
1 John 3:1

"For He chose us in Him before the foundation of the world."
Ephesians 1:4

"He has made peace through the blood of His cross, to present you holy, blameless, and above reproach before Him."
Colossians 1:20–22

"So if the Son sets you free, you will be free indeed."
John 8:36

WHAT THIS CHAPTER HOLDS

This chapter is about false names. The kind that arrive quietly, carried by trauma, loss, rejection, and outcomes you never had the power to change.

Some names were spoken directly to you.
Some were implied through how people treated you.

Some were born in silence because no one stood up, no one intervened, and no one said, "This is wrong."

But every false name has the same assignment: to convince you that what wounded you is who you are.

This chapter is the moment that assignment is refused.

What happened to you may be part of the story, but it is not allowed to become the title.

INTERLUDE: A Name Is an Agreement

A name does more than identify. It positions. It shapes posture, expectation, and permission.

When you accept a name, you begin to live in agreement with it.

"Damaged" teaches you to stay hidden.
"Unchosen" trains you to settle.
"Unworthy" makes you apologize for taking up space.

But Heaven never called you any of those things.

So this chapter is not only remembrance. It is deliverance. It is the moment identity is separated from injury.

A name is an agreement. Today, the wrong ones are broken.

For a long time, I answered to names I never chose.

They were not written on any official document. No one handed them to me directly, at least not at first. They were assigned through experience, pressed into my identity by things I did not invite and outcomes I could not prevent.

Each name carried a weight. Over time, I stopped treating them like descriptions of what I endured and started believing they were definitions of who I was.

Some names came early.

Before I understood what power even was, it was taken from me.

My body was violated before I had language for violation. Molestation taught me a lesson I never consented to learn: that my no could be ignored, that silence could be weaponized, and that my body could be accessed without permission.

Later, rape reinforced that lie with violence. It told me I was disposable, interruptible, and conquerable.

No one stood beside me and named it for what it was. No one said, "This was wrong." No one declared protection out loud.

So the name I answered to became unprotected.

I learned how to disappear without leaving the room. I learned how to leave my body while still breathing.

I learned how to make myself small enough to survive what felt impossible to hold.

Trauma whispered damaged, and for a long time, I agreed.

As I grew older, I tried to outrun those names by building a life that looked stable.

I told myself that if I loved hard enough, committed deeply enough, and gave generously enough, the past would eventually lose its voice.

But pain is patient. It followed me quietly, shaping my expectations, lowering my hope, and instructing my fear.

Marriage became the place where I hoped I would finally be chosen. Divorce became another name.

Twice.

Not once, but twice, I watched vows dissolve. Twice, I felt promises loosen and slip away. Twice, love left.

Each ending reopened the same unspoken question. What is wrong with me?

Why was I not enough to stay for? Why was I chosen and then unchosen? Why was I never number one?

The world did not whisper its conclusions. It labeled me failed, too much, not enough, and hard to love.

And once again, I answered.

I learned to call myself strong, resilient, and independent.

But underneath that strength lived a bone-deep exhaustion, the weariness of constantly proving worth, of outlasting rejection instead of being embraced by permanence.

There was a quiet shame in wondering whether lifelong love was something other people were allowed to have, but not me.

Then there was the grief no one knew how to speak about.

I could not give birth.

That loss did not bleed outward. There were no public goodbyes and no visible wounds. It bled inward, through baby aisles I learned to walk faster through, through smiles practiced at showers and announcements, through tears swallowed whole.

Infertility named me barren, incomplete, and less than.

It suggested my body had failed at something sacred, that it could not do the one thing it was made for.

I watched motherhood celebrated as the pinnacle of womanhood and wondered quietly where that left me.

I loved children. I nurtured deeply. But my arms remained empty in a way words could not touch.

Another name settled in: unfinished.

Through all of this, I became familiar with being overlooked.

Unpreferred.

I noticed it in rooms where my voice was tolerated but never sought. In relationships where I poured more than I received. In seasons where I was loyal, available, and faithful, and still not chosen.

Unpreferred did not always show up dramatically. Sometimes it looked like silence, like being the afterthought, like watching others receive what I had prayed for.

It told me I was acceptable, but never exceptional. Welcome, but never pursued.

And still, I stayed.

Because survival had trained me to treat crumbs like provision.

These names followed me quietly.

Violated.
Divorced.
Childless.
Unchosen.

I wore them like invisible tags, never announcing them, but living as though they were true.

They determined how much space I allowed myself to occupy, how loudly I spoke, and how deeply I hoped.

They taught me to brace instead of expect, to endure instead of desire.

Healing does not begin with denial. It begins with truth.

The truth is this: none of those names were ever mine.

They describe what happened to me, not who I am.

I was not weak because I survived abuse.
I was not defective because my body did not carry life.
I was not unlovable because marriages ended.
I was not insignificant because I was overlooked.

These experiences marked my story, but they do not own my identity.

There came a moment, quiet and unspectacular, when I realized I had been answering voices without authority.

Trauma spoke, but it was not God.
Loss spoke, but it was not truth.
Rejection spoke, but it was not prophecy.

I began, slowly, to lay the names down.

Not all at once.
Not without grief.
But intentionally.

I stopped calling myself what pain had called me.
I stopped agreeing with narratives born from harm.
I stopped letting my worth be measured by outcomes I
could not control.

I am not my violation.
I am not my infertility.
I am not my divorce record.
I am not my history of rejection.

I am a woman who survived what should have broken
her.

I am a woman who loved sincerely, even when love cost
her deeply.

I am a woman whose body tells a story of endurance, not
failure.

I am a woman who remained tender in a world that tried to harden her.

The names I answered to once helped me survive.

They are not the names I live by now.

I am learning to answer to new ones.

Chosen.
Whole.
Beloved.
Seen.

This chapter is not about erasing the past. It is about refusing to let the past name the future.

I carry my story with honesty, not shame.
I honor the girl who endured.
I protect the woman who emerged.

For the first time, when my name is called, I answer as myself.

REFLECTION

Name It / Release It / Replace It

Name it:
What names did pain speak over me, quietly and
repeatedly, that I slowly began to wear like truth?
Which words formed my self image before I ever had
language to challenge them?

Release it:
Which false identity am I still responding to, not because
it is true, but because it is familiar?
Where do my choices, patterns, relationships, or
expectations reveal that I am living as someone I was
never meant to be?

Replace it:
What is God calling me now, not who I was in survival,
not who I became in defense, but who He is forming in
this present season of healing?

Write this truth three times:
What happened to me is not who I am.
What happened to me is not who I am.
What happened to me is not who I am.

JOURNALING PROMPTS

1. The first false name I answered to was
   __________, and it came from __________.

2. The moment I realized it did not belong to me
   was when __________.

3. Rejection trained my heart to believe
   __________ about myself.

4. Loss tried to redefine my future by calling me
   __________.

5. The lie I choose to break agreement with today is
   __________, even though it has felt true for a
   long time.

6. The name God is gently restoring to me now is
   __________, and I am learning how to receive it.

PRAYER

God,
I come to You carrying names I learned to answer to
before I ever knew who I truly was.
Names shaped in moments when I was vulnerable,
unprotected, or unheard.
Names formed by violation, loss, rejection, and silence.

Names that were never spoken out loud, yet still shaped my understanding of worth.

You saw what was done to me when I could not fully protect myself.
You were present when my body was violated and my voice was dismissed.
Nothing was hidden from You, not the pain, not the fear, not the confusion, even when it was hidden from everyone else.

I bring You the places where shame tried to make a home in me.
The moments when pain taught me to disconnect, to endure, to survive instead of truly live.
I release the lie that my trauma defines my value or my identity.

Heal the places in me that learned numbness as a form of safety.
Restore the parts of me that were rushed, silenced, overlooked, or taken too soon.
Reclaim what trauma tried to rename.

I bring You the grief of what never came to be.
The children I could not carry.
The futures I imagined that ended without explanation or closure.
The quiet mourning I held alone because I did not know how to speak it.

Meet me there.
Honor that grief.
Hold it gently without minimizing it and without trying
to explain it away.

I bring You the weight of broken covenants.
The love I gave wholeheartedly that did not remain.
The rejection that taught me to question my worth
instead of the situation itself.

Remove the names I accepted out of exhaustion and
heartbreak.
Failed.
Unchosen.
Unpreferred.

Replace them with truth.
Teach my heart to rest in who You say I am, not in what I
endured.
Where I learned to brace myself, teach me how to trust.
Where I learned to shrink back, teach me how to stand
without apology.

I lay down every false identity formed through pain.
I no longer answer to what violated me, abandoned me,
or overlooked me.
I answer only to Your voice.

Call me whole.
"For He has made peace through the blood of His cross,

to present you holy, blameless, and above reproach
before Him."
Colossians 1:20 through 22

Call me beloved.
"See what great love the Father has lavished on us, that
we should be called children of God, and that is what we
are."
1 John 3:1

Call me chosen.
"For He chose us in Him before the foundation of the
world, that we should be holy and blameless in love."
Ephesians 1:4

Give me the courage to believe You.

Amen.

BREAKING AGREEMENT DECLARATION

Today, I break agreement with the following lies.

- The lie that violation makes me dirty
- The lie that divorce makes me defective
- The lie that infertility makes me incomplete
- The lie that rejection makes me unworthy
- The lie that being overlooked makes me invisible

I cancel every false name.
I silence every accusing voice.
I reject every label rooted in harm.

IDENTITY RESTORATION DECLARATION

I answer to God's voice.

I am chosen.
I am whole.
I am beloved.
I am seen.
I am not behind.
I am not finished.
I am not disqualified.

I answer as myself.
And I belong to God.

Chapter Four

Breaking Agreement With Shame

Key Scriptures

"There is now no condemnation for those who are in Christ Jesus." Romans 8:1

"But You, O Lord, are a shield around me, my glory, and the One who lifts my head." Psalm 3:3

"You did not choose Me, but I chose you and appointed you that you should go and bear fruit, and that your fruit should remain." John 15:16

"The fruit of the Spirit is love, joy, peace…"

Galatians 5:22–23

"The Lord is near to the brokenhearted and saves the crushed in spirit." Psalm 34:18

What This Chapter Holds

Shame is never just a feeling.
Shame is an accusation.

It speaks in verdicts, not whispers. It does not ask questions. It delivers conclusions.

Shame tries to take circumstances you did not choose and turn them into moral failures. It takes limitation and rebrands it as disobedience. It takes grief and reinterprets it as proof.

This chapter is sacred because it confronts a lie many people live beneath for years without ever naming:

God does not measure your faithfulness by what your body could not do.

This chapter breaks the quiet agreement with shame, the one where the soul slowly nods along as it hears: You are behind. You are less than. You are incomplete.

And in its place, truth is restored.

You are loved.
You are whole.
You are fruitful.
You belong.

Interlude: Shame Misuses Scripture

One of shame's most dangerous strategies is that it often sounds religious.

It does not shout in cruelty. It whispers in spiritual language.

"You should have…"
"You didn't do enough…"

"If you were really faithful…"
"If God approved of you, your life would look
different…"

Shame cloaks itself in holiness, but it is not the voice of
God.

God convicts to restore. Shame condemns to collapse.

Conviction says, come closer.
Shame says, stay down.

Conviction lifts the head.
Shame presses it lower.

This chapter is where the difference becomes clear.

Shame rarely announces its arrival. It enters quietly,
dressed as humility and disguised as responsibility. It
convinces you that you missed something sacred, that
your life subtly failed to align with God's expectation.
Once shame settles in, it begins to rewrite how you
understand obedience.

For me, shame attached itself to a single phrase of
Scripture: "Be fruitful and multiply."

Those words were never spoken directly to me, yet they
echoed in my spirit as though they were a personal
command. What was meant as blessing began to sound
like requirement. When my body did not respond the

way I prayed it would, I internalized the outcome as disobedience.

I did not accuse God.
I accused myself.

I wondered how to stand tall in faith when I believed I had failed at something foundational. How could a life glorify God without producing what others called fruit? Shame suggested that I was living in quiet contradiction to God's design, outwardly devoted yet inwardly deficient.

But shame flourishes in misunderstanding.

The command to be fruitful and multiply was spoken within a specific moment and purpose: to a world being formed and to a people being established. It was never a measuring stick for individual worth and never a test of righteousness. God never evaluated faithfulness by fertility.

Still, shame made it personal.

I began to confuse inability with rebellion, limitation with disobedience, and loss with failure.

That confusion seeped into my prayers. I prayed with apology instead of confidence. I spoke to God as though I needed to justify myself, as if He were disappointed or keeping count of what my body could not do.

Shame lowers the eyes.
It makes worship feel complicated.
It makes joy feel undeserved.
It suggests you take up less space in God's presence.

But shame cannot survive truth.

The truth is this: God never holds us responsible for what He did not give us the capacity to do. Scripture consistently distinguishes between obedience and ability. God asks for faithfulness, never outcomes beyond our control.

Jesus Himself redefined fruitfulness. He did not limit it to reproduction. He spoke of fruit as character, love, obedience, endurance, and abiding.

"You did not choose Me, but I chose you and appointed you that you should bear fruit, and that your fruit should remain."

Fruit that remains is not biological.
It is transformative.

Shame told me my life lacked evidence of blessing. God revealed that I was surrounded by it.

I began to see fruit where I once saw absence: in the lives I nurtured, in compassion born of suffering, in wisdom refined by grief, and in faith that endured when hope felt thin.

Shame narrows vision. Grace expands it.

Breaking agreement with shame required confronting the belief that God was disappointed in me. That belief shaped my posture before Him. I approached God guarded and tentative, braced for correction instead of welcome.

Yet Scripture reveals a God who draws nearer to the brokenhearted, not farther away. He is near, not distant. Present, not withholding.

Shame also distorted my understanding of womanhood. I absorbed the belief that value peaked in childbirth and that identity found fulfillment only through reproduction. Scripture never ties a woman's worth to her womb.

God honored women who bore children and women who did not. He called both faithful. He used both powerfully.

Barrenness in Scripture was never a verdict. It was often the place where God revealed His power, His tenderness, and His presence. Even then, the story was never about fertility. It was about faith.

I had to separate God's command from cultural pressure. Culture often weaponizes Scripture, turning blessings into benchmarks and calling it faith. God never asked me to produce what He did not place within me. He asked me to trust Him.

As I broke agreement with shame, my posture changed.

I stopped bowing beneath accusations that did not come from God. I lifted my head, not in pride, but in truth.

How do you hold your head up after believing you failed God?

You lift it by realizing you never disobeyed Him. You lift it by recognizing that God sees the heart, not the outcome. You lift it by understanding that obedience is surrender, not success. You lift it by trusting that God's sovereignty includes your limitations.

Shame told me I needed to explain myself. Grace reminded me that I was already known.

My life was not deficient. It was different. And different does not mean disobedient.

God's command to be fruitful was never meant to crush. It was meant to bless. Blessing does not turn into shame when circumstances change. God's Word does not contradict His compassion.

I stopped asking God to excuse me. I allowed Him to redefine me.

I am fruitful in ways shame refused to acknowledge. I multiply love, wisdom, healing, and faith. I leave legacy in hearts, not just bloodlines.

Breaking agreement with shame did not erase grief. It redeemed it.

There was another place shame once tried to reclaim me.

Rooms filled with women who had given birth. Baby showers. Mother's groups. Conversations layered with milestones and shared knowing. I used to enter those spaces braced, shoulders tight, smile measured, words cautious. Shame whispered that I did not belong, that I was merely an observer, that I should feel smaller where fruit was visible.

But shame was lying.

Holding my head up in those rooms did not require comparison. It required clarity.

I am not intimidated by what God gave to others. Their motherhood does not negate my womanhood, and my story unfolding differently does not diminish their joy.

Honoring their fruit does not require dishonoring my own. I can celebrate birth without feeling erased. I can listen without shrinking. I can stand fully present without explanation.

My confidence is not built on similarity. It is built on belonging.

God did not assign me to those rooms as an outsider. He placed me there as myself, whole, grounded, and secure.

So now, when I walk into those rooms, I lift my head.
Not in defense. Not in pride. But in peace.

I am not less.
I am not behind.
I am not incomplete.

I am present.
I am enough.
And I belong.

REFLECTION

Name It, Release It, Replace It

Name it:
Where has shame tried to quietly rewrite my understanding of obedience, convincing me that faithfulness only counts if it looks a certain way or produces outcomes others can admire?

Release it:
What measuring stick have I been holding myself against that God never placed in my hands, standards rooted in comparison, timelines, or expectations He never required of me?

Replace it:
What fruit is God gently revealing in my life that shame refused to let me see, growth that did not shout, obedience that did not perform, faith that persevered in unseen places?

Truth to repeat:
Different does not mean disobedient.

JOURNALING PROMPTS

1. Shame tried to convince me God was
    disappointed in me because
    _________________________, even when my heart
    was sincere and my obedience costly.

2. I learned to apologize in prayer when
    _________________________, mistaking humility for
    self-erasure.

3. The rooms that used to intimidate me were
    _________________________, places where
    comparison was louder than calling.

4. My new truth about myself is
    _________________________, a truth rooted in how
    God sees me, not how my story compares.

5. I see fruit in my life through
    _________________________, quiet evidence of
    God's faithfulness that continues to mature with
    time.

6. My life multiplies legacy through
    _________________________, seeds planted in
    people, prayers, and perseverance that extend
    beyond what I may ever see.

PRAYER

Heavenly Father,
I come before You with my head lifted, not because my
life unfolded according to my original plans, but because
You have remained faithful through every unexpected
turn.
You are the lifter of my head, just as Your Word declares:
"But You, O Lord, are a shield around me, my glory, and
the One who lifts my head" (Psalm 3:3).

Today, I release every agreement I ever made with
shame, spoken aloud or whispered silently in my heart.
I renounce the lie that says my worth is determined by
outcomes instead of obedience.
Your Word is clear:
"There is now no condemnation for those who are in
Christ Jesus" (Romans 8:1).
I receive that truth, not partially, not cautiously, but fully.

Where I once believed I had failed You, correct my
understanding.
You do not measure my life the way the world does.
You see the heart beneath the effort, the faith beneath the
waiting, the obedience beneath the outcome.
You search me and You know me completely (Psalm
139:1), and nothing about my story surprises or
disappoints You.

Teach me to recognize fruit the way You define it.
Not only in harvest, but in character.
Not only in visibility, but in faithfulness.
Your Word says the fruit of the Spirit is love, joy, peace,
patience, kindness, goodness, faithfulness, gentleness,
and self-control (Galatians 5:22–23).
Let my life overflow with fruit that remains, even when
no one is counting.

When I walk into rooms where comparison once took
root, guard my heart.
Help me rejoice with those who rejoice without
shrinking myself (Romans 12:15).
Remind me that I belong there, not because my story
mirrors theirs, but because You placed me there
intentionally.

Heal the places where grief still echoes.
You are near to the brokenhearted, and You save those
who are crushed in spirit (Psalm 34:18).
Let Your nearness become my confidence, my ground,
my peace.

Replace every lowered gaze with assurance.
You have clothed me with strength and dignity, and I can
face today and every tomorrow without fear (Proverbs
31:25).
I do not enter any space ashamed, intimidated, or
insecure.

I thank You that I am chosen:
"You did not choose Me, but I chose you and appointed you to go and bear fruit" (John 15:16).
I thank You that I am beloved, called Your child (1 John 3:1).
I thank You that I am whole, complete in Christ (Colossians 2:10).

Today, I stand in truth.
I lift my head without apology.
I live free from shame.
And I trust You with my story, my body, my legacy, and my future.

Amen.

"FRUIT THAT REMAINS" DECLARATION

I am not measured by outcomes.
I am measured by faithfulness.

I am fruitful in ways the world cannot calculate or applaud.
I multiply legacy in hearts, not headlines.
I carry wisdom refined through fire.
I nurture what God entrusts to me with care and courage.
And my fruit will remain.

"ROOMS FILLED WITH WOMEN" DECLARATION

When I walk into rooms that once intimidated me,
I lift my head.
I do not shrink.
I do not apologize for being different.
I do not measure myself by standards God never required.

I belong in every space God places me.
I honor their story without dishonoring mine.
I am enough.
I am present.
And I belong.

CHAPTER FOUR CLOSING DECLARATION

Today, I break agreement with shame.

I cancel the lie that says I failed God.
I reject the voice of condemnation.
I silence every measuring stick that did not originate in Heaven.

God's compassion does not contradict His Word.
And His Word does not crush what His love is in the process of healing.

My head is lifted.
My identity is restored.
And I am free.

CHAPTER FIVE

The Weight of Unshed Tears

Key Scriptures

"You have kept count of my tossings; put my tears in
Your bottle. Are they not in Your book?"
Psalm 56:8

"Blessed are those who mourn, for they shall be
comforted."
Matthew 5:4

"Weeping may endure for a night, but joy comes in the
morning."
Psalm 30:5

"Hope deferred makes the heart sick…"
Proverbs 13:12

"Cast your burden on the Lord, and He will sustain you."
Psalm 55:22

What This Chapter Holds

Some tears do not fall because the pain is small.
They do not fall because the pain is unbearable.

Unshed tears are survival tears.
They are the kind you swallow because no one feels safe
enough to witness them.
They are the kind you carry because breaking down feels
like breaking apart.

This chapter honors that version of you, the one who
stayed composed while unraveling inside.
The one who learned how to keep going while quietly
carrying grief that had nowhere to land.

And it gently tells the truth.

Crying is not weakness.
It is release.
It is honesty.
It is healing learning how to breathe again.

Interlude: Tears Require Safety

Tears require permission.
They require safety.
They require a space where falling apart does not cost
you love, stability, or dignity.

So if you could not cry then, it does not mean you did not care.
It means you had no place to rest your sorrow.

And God is not offended by what you had to do to survive.

In this chapter, you are not judged for being strong.
You are invited to stop being strong alone.

The Ache That Never Reached the Surface

There is a kind of pain that never spills outward.
It stays contained, disciplined, managed, and controlled.
These are unshed tears.

They are held back not because the hurt is small, but because releasing it feels dangerous.
When crying feels like something that might undo you instead of heal you.

Scripture gives language to this kind of sorrow.

"My sighing comes instead of my bread, and my groanings are poured out like water."
Job 3:24

Some grief is not dramatic.
Some grief is persistent.
Unshed tears carry weight.

At first, restraint feels like strength.
You tell yourself this is how you survive.
If you can keep your composure, you can keep control.

But unshed tears do not disappear.

They accumulate.
They settle into the chest, the jaw, and the shoulders.
They become pressure behind the eyes, tightness in the throat, and fatigue no amount of rest seems to touch.

They lodge themselves in the places where grief was meant to pass through. Instead, they take up residence.

Learning Not to Cry

There comes a moment, quietly and instinctively, when you learn not to cry.
Not because you do not feel pain, but because there is no one to catch you if you fall apart.

So you adapt.

You teach yourself not to cry.
Not to need.
Not to care too deeply.

When there is no one to depend on, emotion becomes a liability.
Vulnerability requires witness.
Tears require safety.

And when neither is available, restraint becomes survival.

You learn how to keep moving while your heart is breaking.
You learn how to answer questions without telling the truth.
You learn how to swallow emotion mid-breath.

You become skilled at holding devastation behind a calm exterior.

This kind of strength is not born from confidence.
It is born from necessity.

The Cost of Survival

Unshed tears shape the way you move through the world.
They teach you not to expect comfort.
They teach you not to lean.
They convince you that needing anything, whether rest, reassurance, help, or understanding, is weakness.

You become dependable to yourself because no one else was.
You learn to self-soothe.
You learn to endure.

But prolonged suppression does not strengthen the heart.
It wearies it.

Over time, numbness begins to masquerade as peace.
Independence begins to look like maturity, even when it
was forged in abandonment, not empowerment.

Scripture names this truth.

"Hope deferred makes the heart sick."
Proverbs 13:12

You stop hoping because hope once made the fall harder.
You stop caring deeply because caring once cost too
much.
You stop crying because crying once led nowhere.

And yet, God sees even what never surfaced.

"Put my tears in Your bottle. Are they not in Your book?"
Psalm 56:8

Even unshed tears are counted.

When Strength Becomes a Wall

Teaching yourself not to feel is not emotional maturity.
It is emotional triage.

It is what you do when you are bleeding and no one is
there to tend the wound.

But unshed tears come at a cost.

They harden the heart in subtle ways.
They teach it to brace instead of soften.

They create distance, not only from others, but from yourself.

You begin living life cautiously, measuring how much you can afford to feel.

Grief that is not expressed does not disappear.
It waits.

An Invitation to Release

Unshed tears are not a sign of failure.
They are evidence of survival.

But survival was never meant to be the final destination.

The heart was not designed to store sorrow indefinitely.

"Weeping may endure for a night, but joy comes in the morning." Psalm 30:5

Weeping is meant to move through us, not remain trapped within us.

At some point, the heart longs for permission.
Permission to feel without consequence.
Permission to mourn without explanation.
Permission to release without justification.

"Cast your burden on the Lord, and He will sustain you."
Psalm 55:22

That burden includes the tears you never cried.
The grief you postponed so you could keep functioning.

Learning how to cry again may feel unfamiliar.
It may even feel unsafe.

But Scripture does not call us to suppression. It calls us
to honesty.

"Blessed are those who mourn, for they shall be
comforted."
Matthew 5:4

Comfort follows mourning.

Not a Breakdown, But a Return

You were never wrong for surviving the way you did.
You were never weak for holding it together.

But you no longer have to carry everything alone.

And when the tears finally come, whether softly or all at
once, they are not undoing you.
They are returning you to yourself.

They are not a setback.
They are a release.

"He heals the brokenhearted and binds up their wounds."
Psalm 147:3

Even the wounds no one ever saw bleeding.

The weight of unshed tears was never meant to be permanent.

REFLECTION

Name It, Release It, Replace It

Name it:
What did I learn to silence, to shrink, to bury in myself just to make it through another day?
What parts of my heart did I decide were too much, too inconvenient, too unsafe to express?

Release it:
What tears have I pressed back down into my chest because I was afraid of the truth they might expose?
What grief have I delayed because I didn't know who would stay if I finally let it surface?

Replace it:
What would it look like to stop bracing myself and instead allow God to see me fully?
To let Him be my witness, holding my pain with tenderness, instead of my wall, protecting me through isolation?

Truth to repeat:
My tears will not dismantle me.
They will not overwhelm me.
They will not undo me.

My tears will deliver me, into healing, into truth, into
freedom.

JOURNALING PROMPTS

1. The first time I learned "crying isn't safe" was
   ___________.
   What happened in that moment, and what
   conclusion did I draw about my emotions?

2. The emotion I still swallow most often is
   ___________.
   When it rises, what do I tell myself to make it
   disappear?

3. I became self-sufficient because ___________.
   Who wasn't there when I needed them, and how
   did that shape the way I learned to survive?

4. Numbness looks like ___________ in my daily
   life.
   Where do I go blank, distracted, or detached
   instead of present?

5. The kind of comfort I needed but didn't receive
   was ___________.
   If someone had known how to care for me, what
   would they have done differently?

6. If I let myself release, I fear ____________,
    but beneath that fear, I deeply desire

    ____________.

PRAYER

God,
Your Word says in Psalm 147:3 that You heal the
brokenhearted and bind up their wounds.
So I come to You not as someone who has it together, but
as someone who learned to survive by staying quiet.

I bring You the tears I never allowed myself to cry.
The grief I swallowed so I wouldn't be a burden.
The emotions I locked away because there was no one
safe enough to hold them.

You saw every moment I smiled while unraveling inside.
You witnessed the strength I performed and the
exhaustion it concealed.
You counted the nights I lay awake, carrying weight I
didn't know how to set down.

Your Word says in Psalm 56:8 that You keep track of my
tears,
even the ones that pooled behind tired eyes and never
fell.

I confess that I taught myself not to cry, not to need, not
to feel too deeply,
not because I was strong, but because I was alone.

Still, You promise that a bruised reed You will not break,
and a faintly burning wick You will not quench.
So I bring You my fragile places without fear of being
hurried, minimized, or dismissed.

Teach me how to release what I've been holding in my
body and my spirit.
Teach me how to pour out my heart before You and
believe that You are truly my refuge.

Where I hardened myself to survive, soften me gently.
Where I numbed myself to endure, restore my capacity
to feel again.
Your Word declares in Psalm 34:18 that You are near to
the brokenhearted
and that You save those who are crushed in spirit.

So I give You the weight of unshed tears.
I cast this burden onto You, trusting that You will sustain
me.

I receive Your comfort, just as You promised.
I receive the blessing spoken over those who mourn.
Heal what I could not heal.
Bind what I could not tend.
Restore what I thought I would have to carry forever.

I trust You with my heart.
I trust You with my tears, spoken and unspoken.
I trust You with my healing.
Amen.

"RELEASE LITURGY"

God,
I release the tears I postponed so I could function.
I release the grief I swallowed so I wouldn't fall apart.
I release the pain I tucked behind productivity, strength, and achievement.

I give You the words I never found.
I give You the cries I silenced.
I give You the weight I was never meant to carry alone.

And in exchange,
I receive comfort.
I receive tenderness.
I receive healing.

CHAPTER FIVE CLOSING DECLARATION

I do not have to be numb to be safe.
I do not have to be silent to be strong.

God sees every tear, even the ones that never made it to my face.
And when I finally release, I am not unraveling.

I am not breaking down.
I am breaking free.

CHAPTER SIX

THE WEIGHT OF MEMORY

KEY SCRIPTURES

"Forgetting what lies behind and straining forward to what lies ahead…" Philippians 3:13

"Do not remember the former things… Behold, I am doing a new thing." Isaiah 43:18–19

"The old has passed away; behold, the new has come." 2 Corinthians 5:17

"The Lord is near to the brokenhearted…" Psalm 34:18

WHAT THIS CHAPTER HOLDS

Memory itself is not the enemy.
But memory becomes a burden when it is mistaken for identity.

There is a sacred difference between remembering, reliving, and rehearsing.

Some memories were never meant to govern your inner world. They may instruct you. They may warn you. They may even humble you. But they were never meant to rule you.

They can inform you. They cannot define you.

This chapter is about reclaiming your name. About disentangling who you are from what happened. About loosening the grip of the past just enough to breathe again.

INTERLUDE: MEMORY WANTS PERMANENCE

Memory longs for permanence. Healing longs for discernment.

Healing does not erase the past. It simply refuses to let the past author the future.

You are allowed to say:
"That happened. It mattered. It left a mark. But it does not get to name me."

Memory Does Not Knock

Memory does not knock before entering. It slips in quietly, settling into the body long before the mind has language for it. It takes residence in shoulders pulled tight, in jaws clenched without warning, in the space between a laugh and the fear that follows it.

Memory does not always arrive as a story. Sometimes it arrives as tension, as vigilance, as a body that never fully rests.

It becomes weight. Not always crushing, but constant. A familiar heaviness you learn to adjust to, compensate for, and live under. So familiar that one day you forget how it feels to stand without it.

There are memories we treasure. And then there are memories that quietly rename us. Those are heavier.

I did not notice the moment it happened, the shift from survivor to symbol. From a person who lived through something to a person defined by it.

Trauma is patient. It waits until you stop telling the story out loud and then begins telling it for you internally, relentlessly.

Somewhere along the way, my memories stopped being something I carried and became something I was.

I was the girl who went through that.
I was the one who survived this.

My identity was eclipsed by my endurance. And without realizing it, my real name faded beneath the weight of memory.

When Memory Becomes a Name

The mind is a meticulous archivist. It catalogs not only what happened, but how it felt to be unseen, powerless, and unprotected.

It remembers tone, temperature, and silence.

It remembers the precise moment something essential cracked. Not always loudly, but often through quiet conclusions.

This is not safe.
This is not fair.
No one is coming to fix this.

Memory is not merely recall. It is rehearsal.

It replays scenes we did not consent to rewatch. It asks questions with no answers. It scans every new relationship for familiar threats.

Will this end like before?
Will I be disappointed again?
Will this kindness vanish?

Gradually, memory learns to speak in the grammar of identity.

You are the abandoned one.
You are the damaged one.

You are the overlooked one.
You are the mistake.

The danger is not that these things happened, but that we begin to believe they are the truest things about us.

I wore my memories like credentials. Proof of resilience. Proof of pain tolerance. Proof that I had earned the right to stay guarded.

Survival shaped me, but it also exhausted me. No one teaches you that surviving something does not automatically mean you stop living inside it.

The Body Remembers What the Mouth Releases

Even when I stopped speaking about it, my body kept the record.

My shoulders learned to brace.
My breath learned to remain shallow.
My heart learned to expect loss.

I flinched at gentleness because memory told me it was temporary. I mistrusted joy because memory promised it would be taken. I rehearsed grief in advance and called it wisdom.

But it was not wisdom. It was armor. And armor is heavy.

Memory trained my reactions before my choices could intervene. I prepared for pain even in neutral rooms. I mistook vigilance for safety.

So I lived prepared. Prepared to be hurt. Prepared to be left. Prepared to be misunderstood.

Prepared, but never truly free.

What Happened to Me Is Not Who I Am

This sentence is the one memory resists most. Memory demands permanence. It wants loyalty. It wants the past to remain relevant forever.

There is comfort in familiar pain. Releasing it feels like betrayal, as though letting go diminishes the wrongness of what happened.

For a long time, I believed healing meant erasure. That moving forward required pretending it did not matter.

But healing is not amnesia. Healing is distinction.

It is learning to say:
This happened to me, but it is not me.
This marked a chapter, not the title.
This shaped me, but it does not name me.

The weight of memory loosens not through denial, but through dethronement.

The Names We Carry

Names tell stories before we speak.

Memory tried to rename me. Broken. Damaged. Too much. Not enough.

And I answered.

I answered with silence when my voice mattered. With over explaining when rest was deserved. With self blame because it felt familiar.

The most dangerous lie memory tells is that the worst thing that happened to you is the most honest thing about you.

But my name is not what they did. My name is not what I lost. My name is not what I endured.

My name is not!

Learning to Lay It Down

There comes a quiet moment, not dramatic and not public, when the body grows tired before the mind does. Not tired of living, but tired of carrying.

For me, it was not a breakthrough. It was a surrender.

I stopped asking memory to justify my pain. I stopped rehearsing explanations for wounds that no longer

needed defending. I stopped inviting the past into rooms
it no longer belonged in.

I did not forget. I did not excuse. I did not erase.

I set boundaries.

I said, you may inform me, but you may not define me.
You may visit, but you may not live here.

Slowly, the weight shifted. It did not disappear, but it
redistributed. No longer crushing my chest, it settled into
my hands, where I could choose what to carry and what
to release.

The Courage to Become

Survival is brave. Becoming is braver.

Becoming asks you to risk joy without guarantees. To
trust yourself more than your memories. To believe there
is more ahead than behind.

I am still learning how to remember without reliving.
How to honor my story without surrendering my future
to it. How to speak the past without allowing it to speak
for me.

Memory still whispers, but it no longer commands. And
when it tries to name me, I answer back.

You are not my identity.
You are not my destiny.
You are not my name.

The weight of memory is real. It teaches, humbles, and shapes us. But it was never meant to replace us.

You are not what happened to you.
You are not the name pain gave you.
You are not the sum of your hardest moments.

You are more than memory. And if you listen closely, beneath the echoes of what was, you may hear your true name returning.

REFLECTION

Name It, Release It, Replace It

Name it:
What memory presses hardest against my chest when I am finally ready to move forward?
Which moment rises uninvited, raising its voice just as I gather the courage to step into more?

Release it:
What quiet rehearsal do I keep running in my mind, the imagined failure, the old ending, the familiar hurt, that keeps me braced for impact instead of open to possibility?

Replace it:
What truer story can I practice instead of pain?
What living, breathing truth deserves repetition in place of fear?

Truth to repeat:
Memory may visit, but it may not live here.
It passes through, but it does not get the keys.

JOURNALING PROMPTS

1. A memory that still tries to name me is
    __________, the one that whispers who I used to
    be when I forget who I am becoming.

2. My body remembers through __________, the
    tightening, the shallow breath, the sudden
    silence, the instinct to disappear.

3. I rehearse the worst because __________, some
    part of me still believes preparedness equals
    survival.

4. I want to remember without reliving by
    __________, choosing compassion over self-
    punishment and grounding myself in the present.

5. I am setting this boundary with memory:
    __________. You may speak, but you no longer
    decide my direction.

6. Becoming looks like __________ for me, small
    brave steps, softer self-talk, and trust that growth
    does not require suffering.

DECLARATION: YOU MAY INFORM ME

Memory, you may inform me, but you will not define me.

You may visit, but you will not take up residence in my thoughts.

You may remind, but you will not rule my decisions.

My past is a chapter.
Not the title.
Not the prophecy.
Not my name.

BREATH PRAYER

Inhale: God, You are here.
Exhale: I return to now.

Inhale: You are restoring what was fractured.
Exhale: I release the endless replay.

Inhale: I am safe today, in this moment.
Exhale: I do not have to relive what is over.

Inhale: My name is held in You.
Exhale: I am more than what I remember.

CHAPTER SIX, CLOSING DECLARATION

I honor what I survived, the resilience it required and the strength it revealed, but I refuse to be imprisoned by it.

I remember with wisdom, not weight.
I speak with truth, not trauma.
I step forward with courage, not rehearsal.

And when memory tries to name me, when it attempts to speak louder than my present, I answer back:

You are not my identity.
You are not my destiny.
You are not my name.

CHAPTER SEVEN

BEYOND WHAT HELD ME

KEY SCRIPTURES

"Where the Spirit of the Lord is, there is freedom."
2 Corinthians 3:17

"God has not given us a spirit of fear, but of power and of love and of a sound mind." 2 Timothy 1:7

"You enlarged my steps under me, and my feet did not slip." Psalm 18:36

"The Lord will perfect that which concerns me."
Psalm 138:8

WHAT THIS CHAPTER HOLDS

Sometimes pain does not arrive as a cage.
Sometimes it arrives as shelter.

You did not become smaller because you were weak.
You became smaller because the space you were in required it.

This chapter is about the moment your soul realizes the truth.
The container that once guarded you is now limiting you.

Healing is not reckless expansion.
It is sacred growth, God gently widening the boundaries

around your heart until your spirit has room to breathe
again.

INTERLUDE

CONTAINMENT IS NOT CALLING

Containment teaches you how to survive narrow places.
Calling teaches you how to live in wide ones.

Containment whispers, don't feel too deeply.
Calling invites, tell the whole truth.

Containment warns, don't hope too boldly.
Calling urges, stretch again.

Containment says, stay small to stay safe.
Calling promises, God will enlarge you.

This chapter is your permission to stop mistaking walls
for wisdom and begin stepping into the open.

Beyond What Held Me

Pain rarely announces itself as a prison.
More often, it enters quietly as protection.

In the beginning, containment feels intelligent,
responsible, necessary.
You learn how to survive by shrinking, by folding sharp
edges inward so the pain does not cut everything it
touches. You learn what parts of yourself can be shown
and what must be hidden. Which emotions are

acceptable. Which griefs are too loud. Which questions are too dangerous.

You master the skill of appearing functional.
You keep moving. You keep producing. You keep showing up.
Containment keeps you alive.

But it was never meant to become your home.

The Story of the Snake

There is something hauntingly symbolic about the boa constrictor.
When raised in captivity, a boa does not grow beyond the size of its enclosure. The walls do not force it to stop. The ceiling does not press down on its body. Instead, the snake adapts. Its growth quietly conforms to the limits of its environment.

The container teaches the body how much space it is allowed to take.

But a boa in the wild tells a different story.
In open terrain, unrestricted and expansive, it grows to its intended length. Its muscles thicken. Its power develops. Its size reflects the freedom it inhabits.

Same species.
Different environment.
A drastically different destiny.

This is how pain shapes people.

How We Learn to Shrink

When trauma enters your life, you don't just endure it.
You contain it.
You compress it into quiet places, the tightness in your
chest, the lump in your throat, the constant ache behind
your ribs.

You tell yourself, I'll deal with this later.
You tell yourself, others have it worse.
You tell yourself, I can't fall apart right now.

So you survive.

What no one teaches you is this. The version of you that
grows inside containment adapts to the walls around it.
And adaptation is not healing.

Containment trains you to be careful with your own
needs.
Don't feel too much.
Don't want too much.
Don't expect too much.

You regulate your pain by regulating your hope.
You lower your expectations for joy.
You make your dreams smaller because smaller dreams
hurt less when they collapse.

Like the captive snake, you stop stretching toward space
you're not sure exists.

Strength in Small Spaces

And still, there is strength here.

You become resilient in tight places.
Observant. Controlled. Self sufficient.
You learn how to coil instead of expand, how to brace
instead of rest.

From the outside, it looks like maturity.
From the inside, it feels like suffocation.

Worst of all, over time, you forget there was ever
anything beyond the walls.

When Containment Becomes a Cage

There is a moment, quiet but unmistakable, when what
once protected you begins to restrain you.

You notice it when joy feels unfamiliar.
When rest makes you anxious.
When love feels like pressure instead of safety.

You notice it when small moments provoke oversized
reactions.
When old pain bleeds into new situations.
When exhaustion follows you, not because life is

demanding, but because you are still holding everything together with clenched fists.

Pain that is never released does not disappear.
It compresses.
It hardens.
It finds other exits, anger, numbness, withdrawal, self sabotage.

Your soul knows the truth before your mind does.
You were designed for more space than this.

Breaking the Walls

Breaking containment is not reckless. It is essential.
But it is terrifying.

The walls you built were familiar, predictable.
They gave you control.
Stepping beyond them feels like exposure, like nakedness, like danger.

In the wild, the boa must relearn movement.
No glass. No guarantees. No controlled conditions.

Freedom requires strength that captivity never asked for.
So does healing.

To break containment is to let pain breathe.
To name what happened without softening the edges.
To let grief occupy the space it was always owed.

Survival was not the destination.
It was the doorway.

The Fear of Expansion

Beneath containment lives a quiet terror.
If I let myself grow, will I lose control?

We fear that if the door opens, everything we've held
back will flood out and consume us. That the pain will
be too vast, too heavy, too demanding.

But pain does not destroy you when it is released.
It overwhelms you when it is suppressed.

Expansion does not create chaos.
Expansion creates capacity.

The wild does not weaken the snake.
It completes it.

You were never fragile.
You were constrained.

Learning to Live Uncontained

Uncontained living is not reckless living.
It is truthful living.

It is telling your story without apology.
It is allowing yourself to feel without self judgment.
It is letting your narrative stretch beyond survival into
purpose.

You stop asking, how do I keep this together?
And begin asking, who am I becoming beyond this?

You build emotional muscle you never needed in
captivity.
Discernment. Resilience. Trust.

You learn that pain acknowledged loses its power to
govern you.
You learn that space does not erase wounds.
It gives them room to heal.

You were never meant to remain coiled.

From Contained to Called

The captive snake survives.
The wild snake fulfills its design.

Containment kept you alive.
But freedom is what allows you to become.

Breaking containment is not forgetting what happened.
It is refusing to let it define the size of your future.

You were never too much.
You were never wrong for wanting more air.

You were simply living inside walls you have now
outgrown.

Pain was never meant to be your enclosure.
Hurt was never meant to define your limits.
And survival was never meant to be your ceiling.

Let God widen your steps.
Let your soul take up space.
Break the containment.

REFLECTION

Name It

Where did I first learn that shrinking was the safest way to survive?
Who taught me, directly or quietly, that being fully seen might cost me something I could not afford to lose?

Release It

What invisible container am I still living inside?
Where have I mistaken familiarity for safety and limitation for wisdom?
What space is God gently calling me beyond, even if it feels unfamiliar at first?

Replace It

What would it truly look like to expand with care, with discernment, and with faith?
How might growth feel when it is rooted in truth rather than driven by fear?

Truth to Repeat

I was never too much.
I was not wrong, excessive, or overwhelming.
I was simply contained in places that could not hold the fullness of who I am.

JOURNALING PROMPTS

1. My emotional container looks like a set of expectations, unspoken rules, or protective habits that once kept me safe but now keep me small.

2. I learned to coil when I realized that expressing myself brought discomfort, rejection, or misunderstanding.

3. The wall I built helped me by protecting my heart and preserving my strength, but it limits me by restricting my growth and muting my voice.

4. The truth I am ready to name out loud is that I am allowed to take up space and still be secure.

5. One way I will practice expansion this week is by choosing honesty instead of silence, presence instead of withdrawal, or trust instead of fear.

DECLARATION

BREAK THE CONTAINMENT

I break the containment.
I break the ceiling I learned to live under.
I break the quiet agreement that told me staying small was the price of peace.

God is enlarging me.
God is widening my steps and strengthening my footing.
God is restoring my capacity to feel, to hope, and to fully live.

I do not coil forever.
I expand in truth and integrity.
I grow in peace that does not depend on hiding.

BREATH PRAYER

Inhale. God, enlarge me.
Exhale. I release the walls I no longer need.

Inhale. I was created for more.
Exhale. I step beyond survival and into life.

Inhale. You are with me here.
Exhale. I allow myself to take up space.

CLOSING DECLARATION

Survival was never my ceiling.
Pain was never meant to be my enclosure.
I am called beyond what once held me together by fear.

And I will grow in the open places God provides,
with courage, with wisdom, and with grace.

Chapter 8

The Wall That Pain Built

Key Scriptures

"He heals the brokenhearted and binds up their wounds." Psalm 147:3

"I will give you a new heart and put a new spirit within you." Ezekiel 36:26

"When I am afraid, I will trust in You." Psalm 56:3

"Perfect love drives out fear." 1 John 4:18

What This Chapter Holds

Walls are not built because you wanted to be distant or unfeeling. They are built because, at some point, you needed to be safe. You learned how to survive in the absence of protection. You learned how to guard what was tender when no one else did.

But walls do not only block pain. They also block love. They dull softness. They mute hope. What once preserved you can slowly begin to imprison you.

This chapter honors the wall. It acknowledges what it protected and why it existed. Then, without shame or force, it begins to loosen the bricks. One by one. Gently. Intentionally.

Interlude: The Wall Was a Response

The wall was never who you were. It was a response to what happened to you.

It formed when apologies never came. When prayers felt unanswered. When disappointment became familiar. When safety was inconsistent and trust felt risky.

Your body learned to adapt. Your mind learned to armor itself. Your heart learned how to brace for impact.

This chapter is not about blaming yourself for building the wall. It is about recognizing that you are no longer who you were when it was constructed. You are stronger now. Safer now. And ready, if you choose, to let it come down.

Pain does not announce when it begins to build. It arrives quietly and lays its foundation slowly. One disappointment becomes another. A failure follows close behind. A betrayal goes unresolved. A prayer rises and never seems to return with an answer. Over time, without noticing, a wall stands where tenderness once lived.

That wall was not built from bitterness. It was built from necessity. Pain taught you how to protect yourself when healing felt unavailable. Trauma taught you how to survive when safety was unpredictable. The wall is evidence that you endured. Yet walls do more than keep pain out. They also keep truth out. And if left standing too long, they become the voice that responds to everything before you do.

How Trauma Teaches the Body to Remember

Trauma is not only something you remember. It is something your body carries. It exists beyond logic. Before your mind can reason, your body reacts. A tone of voice. A familiar expression. A situation that echoes the past. Suddenly your heart races. Your chest tightens. Your spirit pulls inward.

Triggers are not signs of weakness. They are echoes of moments when you were hurt without control. Moments when you trusted and paid the price. Moments when hope felt foolish in hindsight.

Trauma trains the nervous system to remain alert. To anticipate loss. To assume disappointment. Each time your body says, "I will not be caught off guard again," the wall becomes stronger. You grow careful and measured. Not because you lack faith, but because faith once cost you something.

The Accumulation of Unresolved Pain

Not all pain arrives in one devastating moment. Some of the deepest wounds are formed through repetition. Repeated rejection. Repeated failure. Repeated disappointment. You tried again. You prayed again. You hoped again. And still you were left feeling unseen.

Every unresolved hurt adds another layer to the wall. Every unanswered question strengthens it. Every time you told yourself it did not matter when it truly did. Eventually, the wall grows so familiar that you forget what life felt like before it existed.

Love begins to feel unsafe. Joy feels fleeting. Expectations feel dangerous. So you stop expecting. You stop reaching. You stop risking. Not because you do not want more, but because you do not want to hurt again.

When the Wall Answers Before You Do

The danger of unresolved pain is not only that it remains. It is that it begins to speak for you. When pain goes unhealed, it interprets every experience. The wall responds before you can consider another possibility.

Someone disappoints you, and the wall insists it was inevitable. Someone offers closeness, and the wall warns against trusting it. Something good starts to form, and the wall predicts its end before it has time to grow.

Pain becomes the translator of reality. Without healing, you are no longer responding to the present. You are reacting to the past.

Failures That Still Shape the Inner Voice

Failure leaves marks when it is never processed. Perhaps you failed in ways others saw. Perhaps only you know. You may have tried sincerely and still fallen short. Instead of being met with grace, that moment became a label.

The wall remembers. It reminds you of who you were at your lowest. It replays mistakes when you consider something new. It tells you growth will not last and that regression is inevitable. So you hesitate. You second guess. You stay small.

Not because you lack ability, but because pain taught you how to see yourself. When healing is absent, failure begins to sound prophetic.

Disappointment With God That Often Goes Unspoken

Some walls exist between you and people. Others exist between you and God. You prayed and believed, and it still did not happen. You obeyed, and it still hurt. You trusted, and it still fell apart.

Disappointment with God is rarely named, but it is deeply felt. When it remains unacknowledged, it turns into distance. You still believe, but you no longer expect. You still worship, but you quietly avoid hope.

The wall whispers caution. Do not trust too much. Do not ask for too much. Do not hope too deeply. Pain starts answering your prayers before heaven does.

The Illusion of Safety

The wall feels protective, and for a time, it truly is. It prevents open bleeding. It reduces surprise. It keeps emotions controlled and expectations low.

But safety without healing becomes confinement. The wall cannot tell the difference between danger and possibility. It blocks both. Love remains at a distance. Growth stays just out of reach.

Eventually, what once protected you begins to limit you. You survive, but you do not fully live.

Deliverance Is Not Forgetting

Deliverance does not mean pretending the past never happened. It means the past no longer dictates the present. Healing does not erase the story. It redeems the voice that tells it.

As healing comes, triggers lose authority. Memories lose control. The wall begins to shift. Not through force, but through intention. Brick by brick.

Deliverance teaches you how to respond instead of react. To discern instead of defend. To hope without abandoning wisdom. You begin to say, "That hurt me, but it does not lead me."

Letting the Wall Come Down Carefully

Walls do not fall safely when rushed. God does not dismantle what pain constructed without care. He removes bricks where truth can now support what fear once held together.

Healing looks like awareness before change. Naming before release. Honesty before freedom. It begins by acknowledging the wall's existence and appreciating how it once helped you.

You do not lower it to become exposed. You lower it to become free.

When Pain No Longer Answers First

The turning point is often quiet. It is the pause before reacting. The moment you question the instinct to protect yourself automatically. The realization that unfamiliar does not always mean unsafe.

When pain no longer answers first, truth finally has room to speak. You see more clearly. You trust more wisely. You hope with balance. You stop living from what hurt you and start living from what healed you.

The Wall Does Not Get the Final Word

The wall pain built was never meant to last forever. It was a shelter, not a home. A response, not an identity. A season, not a sentence.

Deliverance does not erase who you were. It restores where you are going.

And when the wall finally comes down, you realize something sacred. You were never weak for building it. You are strong enough now to let it go. Pain no longer answers for you.

Healing does.

And this time, the response is freedom.

REFLECTION

Name It, Release It, Replace It

Name It:
What was the very first brick laid in my wall, the
moment I learned it was safer to guard than to feel?
Was it betrayal that cracked trust open?
Repetition that wore hope thin?
Abandonment that taught me not to expect anyone to
stay?
Or disappointment that whispered, "Don't reach too far
again."

Release It:
Where do I notice the wall responding before I have time
to choose?
When does my body brace before my heart speaks?
Where does defensiveness answer faster than truth, and
withdrawal faster than vulnerability?

Replace It:
What would it look like if truth answered first, before
fear, before memory, before self protection?
What if honesty, not hurt, shaped my response?
What if love did not have to fight its way through stone?

Truth to Repeat:
Pain is not my translator anymore.

It no longer gets to interpret my reality or speak on my behalf.

JOURNALING PROMPTS

1. My wall protected me from ___________, from breaking, from hoping, from needing, from reliving what once wounded me.

2. My wall also blocked ___________, connection, intimacy, softness, joy, God's nearness.

3. A trigger that echoes the past is ___________, and it pulls old memories into the present moment without asking permission.

4. My disappointment with God has sounded like ___________, silence, unanswered prayers, confusion, or unmet expectations.

5. The brick God is removing first is ___________, the one I thought I needed most, but that no longer serves healing.

6. A safer response I want to practice is ___________, pausing, breathing, naming the fear, choosing honesty over retreat.

DECLARATION

"Brick by Brick"

God, remove the wall carefully.
Brick by brick.
With patience, not pressure.
With gentleness, not force.

Without rushing my healing.
Without shaming my survival.

I release hypervigilance, the constant scanning for
danger.
I release the need to brace for impact.
I release the fear of hoping again and being disappointed.

Truth will answer first.
Not fear. Not memory. Not old pain.
Healing will lead now.

BREATH PRAYER

Inhale: God, You are near.
Exhale: I soften what I have held tight.

Inhale: You heal the brokenhearted.
Exhale: I release the wall, even if slowly.

Inhale: I can pause before reacting.
Exhale: I choose truth over instinct.

CLOSING DECLARATION

The wall helped me survive a season.
But it will not lead my life.

Pain will not answer for me anymore.
The past will not interpret my present.

Healing speaks now.
And the response is freedom.

If you want, I can also adapt this for spoken delivery,
devotional formatting, or print layout.

Chapter Nine

Unveiling Your True Potential

Key Scriptures

"For we are His workmanship, created in Christ Jesus for good works." Ephesians 2:10

"For I know the plans I have for you."
Jeremiah 29:11

"Do not despise these small beginnings."
Zechariah 4:10

"Now to Him who is able to do immeasurably more."
Ephesians 3:20

What This Chapter Holds

Potential is not something you earn. It is not a reward for perfection, performance, or perseverance. Potential is something you uncover. It has always belonged to you.

This chapter marks a deep internal shift. It is the movement from a survival based identity into purpose driven alignment. You are not attempting to prove your worth. You are learning how to live without interference.

Healing does not create something new within you. Healing removes what has been covering you. Truth does not manufacture purpose. Truth reveals what was always there.

Interlude: Survival Traits Are Not Your Name

Survival taught you how to adapt. It taught you how to read the room, anticipate danger, perform when necessary, and brace yourself for uncertainty. It taught you how to be useful, dependable, and strong even when you were exhausted.

Those traits helped you endure seasons that might otherwise have broken you. They served a purpose. But they are not the whole of who you are.

This chapter invites a courageous question. What would your life look like if you lived from alignment instead of approval. What would change if you no longer asked what was expected of you, but asked what was true.

Potential is not something you acquire. It is something you uncover.

For a long time, your truest self, lived beneath layers you did not choose. Expectations were placed on you. Trauma shaped your reactions. Roles formed around necessity. Survival strategies wrapped themselves so tightly around your identity that you began to mistake them for your essence. You learned how to function, how to manage, how to endure. But you did not always learn how to fully emerge.

This chapter is not about becoming someone new. It is about remembering who you were before the world told you who to be.

The Difference Between Survival and Identity

Survival is adaptive, but identity is inherent. When life demanded resilience, you responded by becoming whatever the moment required. You learned how to be strong when you wanted rest. Quiet when you wanted to speak. Reliable when you needed support. Invisible when visibility felt unsafe.

These traits kept you alive. They protected you. But they were never meant to define the full expression of your design.

Over time, survival traits can harden into identity statements. You may have learned to say, "I am the strong one." Or, "I do not need help." Or, "I am not creative." Or even, "I am not chosen." These are not truths. They are accommodations.

Your potential has remained intact beneath them, waiting patiently for permission to surface.

How Limitation Becomes Familiar

Limitation often feels safe because it is predictable. You know what it is like to stay small. You know how to manage disappointment without being undone by it. You know how to operate within emotional limits that minimize risk and exposure.

Growth, however, feels unfamiliar. And unfamiliar can feel dangerous to someone who has survived by control and certainty.

So potential is postponed. Not because you lack capacity, but because expansion threatens the structures you built to stay intact. Unveiling your true potential requires confronting the belief that comfort equals safety. Sometimes the walls that protected you are the same walls that are now confining you.

The Role of Healing in Revealing Potential

Unhealed pain distorts self perception. It whispers that your past disqualifies you. It convinces you that your mistakes define your ceiling. It suggests that your wounds limit your usefulness.

Healing restores clarity. As pain loosens its grip, your vision sharpens. You begin to notice talents you ignored or dismissed. Desires you buried because they felt impractical or unreachable. Callings you silenced because you did not feel ready or qualified.

Healing does not add anything to you. It removes the interference. What was always present finally becomes visible.

Reclaiming What You Silenced

At some point, you stopped listening to parts of yourself.
Perhaps your voice was dismissed. Perhaps your dreams
were labeled unrealistic. Perhaps your authenticity was
inconvenient for others.

So you adapted. You quieted the parts of you that felt too
emotional, too creative, too intense, or too hopeful. Over
time, silence became second nature.

Potential often hides in what you learned to suppress.
The creativity you abandoned. The leadership you
downplayed. The compassion you restrained to avoid
disappointment. Unveiling your true potential means
allowing those parts of you to speak again without
shame or apology.

Letting Go of Borrowed Labels

Labels carry weight, especially when they come from
authority, trauma, or repeated experience. Words like
failure, average, difficult, or unworthy can lodge
themselves deeply within the soul.

When held long enough, labels begin to shape choices,
relationships, and ambition. They create ceilings that feel
logical but are entirely artificial.

Your name is not the labels that were assigned to you.
Your identity is not the conclusions others reached based

on limited understanding. Releasing borrowed labels creates sacred space for authentic self definition.

Potential Requires Responsibility

Potential is not passive. Once it is revealed, it asks something of you. It requires courage to step forward. Discipline to remain consistent. Responsibility to steward what you have been given.

Unveiling your true potential does not produce instant fulfillment. It produces intentional alignment. You begin making choices that reflect who you are becoming, not who you were trying to protect.

This shift is subtle but powerful. You stop waiting for permission. You stop shrinking to preserve relationships. You stop betraying yourself for acceptance. Potential grows where it is honored.

The Fear of Being Seen

One of the greatest barriers to potential is visibility. Being seen invites judgment, expectation, and accountability. It removes the safety of obscurity.

For someone who has lived in survival, this can feel overwhelming. But hiding does not preserve peace. It postpones purpose.

Unveiling your true potential requires accepting that visibility is not exposure. It is expression. You are not revealing your flaws. You are revealing your function.

Living From Alignment, Not Approval

When your life is aligned with your true self, approval becomes secondary. Feedback may inform you, but it no longer defines you. Resistance may arise, but it no longer deters you.

Alignment creates internal stability that external opinion cannot shake. This is freedom. You move with clarity instead of comparison. With intention instead of insecurity. With confidence rooted in congruence, not applause.

The Unveiling Is Ongoing

Unveiling your true potential is not a single moment. It is a continuing process. Each season removes another layer. Each healed wound reveals another capacity. Each courageous decision draws you closer to full expression.

You are not late.
You are not behind.
You are not lacking.

You are unfolding.

Becoming Who You Already Are

The greatest revelation is this. Your potential was never missing. It was hidden beneath pain, fear, obligation, and expectation, yet it remained untouched and whole.

As you release what no longer fits, what remains feels familiar. Not foreign, but true.

You are not reinventing yourself. You are returning to yourself.

And in that return, your life begins to reflect the depth, purpose, and power that were always there, patiently waiting to be unveiled.

REFLECTION

Name It, Release It, Replace It

Name it.
What survival trait have I been carrying so long that I mistook it for who I am? What pattern once kept me safe but now limits my becoming?

Release it.
What label am I finally willing to lay down, knowing it no longer tells the truth about me and no longer gets to define my future?

Replace it.
What aligned, embodied action can I take this week that honors who I truly am and supports the life I am growing into?

Truth to repeat.
Visibility is not exposure. It is expression. It is the courage to be seen as I truly am, without apology or fear.

JOURNALING PROMPTS

1. I learned to stay small when safety depended on silence and shrinking felt like protection.

2. A label I have internalized is one that once explained me but now confines me.

3. The part of me I silenced is the voice that knew, felt deeply, and dared to want more.

4. If I lived from alignment, I would move with integrity, choose myself without guilt, and trust what God placed inside me.

5. One courageous step I will take is a choice that honors truth over comfort and growth over approval.

DECLARATION: I AM UNFOLDING

I am not late.
I am not behind.
I am unfolding in divine timing.

I release the labels that were never mine to carry.
I embrace aligned living with intention and faith.
I steward what God has revealed, even when it stretches me.

I will not hide my function or dim my light.
I will not shrink my calling to make others comfortable.

I will not betray myself for approval, acceptance, or
belonging.

BREATH PRAYER

Inhale. God, reveal what is true within me.
Exhale. I release the labels that no longer serve me.

Inhale. I am Your workmanship, created with purpose.
Exhale. I step forward into that purpose with trust.

DECLARATION

My potential was never missing.
It was covered by fear, survival, and misunderstanding.

As healing clears the interference, I return to myself.
I arrive whole, prepared, and aligned, ready to live fully
as who I was always meant to be.

Chapter Ten
TRIGGERS AND TRAUMAS

Trauma is not only something that happened.
It is something that stayed.

It settled quietly into my body, lingering long after the moment had passed. It showed up in the way I flinched without warning. In how I instinctively braced myself before anything even went wrong. It lived in the way my stomach clenched at certain tones of voice, or how my chest grew heavy when a room fell silent. It appeared when my thoughts raced ahead, rehearsing a thousand possible endings before a moment had even begun to unfold.

This is how trauma trains you.
It teaches you to live ahead of yourself, always preparing for impact.

A trigger is not always loud or obvious. Most of the time, it is subtle and unassuming.
It can be a familiar smell that pulls the breath from your lungs.
A song that tightens your throat.
A look that feels loaded with meaning.
A particular kind of silence that feels unsafe.
A raised voice.
A closed door.
A delayed response.

Being ignored.
Being questioned.
Being interrupted.
Being misunderstood.

And suddenly, without consent or warning, I was no longer in the present.

I was back in the past emotionally, not because I wanted to be there, but because my body learned how to return there quickly. It learned that speed could mean survival.

When the Past Shows Up in the Present

A trigger is the moment the past reaches into the now and whispers, "See, it's happening again."

It does not matter that the person standing in front of you is different.
It does not matter that the circumstances have changed.
It does not matter that logic says you are safe.

What matters is the feeling.

Trauma does not speak the language of reason.
It speaks through sensation.
It recognizes danger through similarity, not truth.

When you have lived through pain that rewired your sense of safety, your body becomes a guard dog. It is always alert, always listening, always scanning for the sound of harm, even in places that look peaceful.

The Body Remembers

My body remembered everything, even when I tried not to.

My mind told me I was moving forward.
My faith tried to speak reassurance over fear.
My smile tried to convince the world, and sometimes myself, that I was fine.

But the body keeps its own record.

Trauma lives in the nervous system. It reshapes breathing. It disrupts sleep. It dulls or sharpens appetite. It scatters concentration. It complicates trust. And without warning, something ordinary can suddenly feel like a threat.

That is what made triggers so exhausting. Not the moment itself, but the internal reaction that felt far bigger than the moment ever deserved to be.

Triggers Do Not Mean I Am Not Healed

For a long time, I believed that being triggered meant I was failing.

I told myself that if I were truly healed, I would not react this way.
If I were truly free, I would not feel this.
If I were truly strong, I would not be bothered.

But healing is not the absence of triggers.
Healing is what happens after the trigger arrives.

Healing means I do not abandon myself when my body
panics.
Healing means I refuse to shame myself for feeling.
Healing means I learn how to return to the present
without punishment or self contempt.

Triggers do not mean I am not healed.
They mean that there is a part of me asking for
gentleness.

How Trauma Reinterprets the World

Trauma changes how you interpret what is happening
around you.

Neutral moments begin to feel dangerous.
A delayed text feels like abandonment.
A correction feels like rejection.
A boundary feels like betrayal.
A disagreement feels like loss.

Trauma turns discomfort into doom, not because you are
dramatic, but because your system learned that endings
hurt and it will do almost anything to avoid reliving that
pain.

The Lie Behind the Trigger

Behind every trigger, there is a lie trying to prove itself
true.

Being ignored whispers, "I do not matter."
Being corrected mutters, "I am not enough."
Being abandoned insists, "I am unlovable."
Being yelled at declares, "I am not safe."
Being misunderstood claims, "I am alone."

Healing begins when you recognize that the trigger itself
is real, but the lie it carries is not.

How I Learned to Come Back to Myself

One of the greatest breakthroughs in my healing was
understanding this simple truth.
I am not required to react.

I can pause.
I can breathe.
I can name what is happening.

I learned to tell myself, "This is a trigger, not a
prophecy."
"This is an echo, not the truth."
"This is my nervous system trying to protect me."

Slowly, I began to build a new path inside myself.

Instead of moving from trigger to panic to reaction to shame, I practiced something different. I moved from trigger to pause, to naming, to grounding, to truth. Each time I did it, the path became easier to find.

God Heals the Root, Not Just the Response

God does not only heal behavior.
He heals bruises beneath the surface.
He heals memory.
He heals the moment that taught you to flinch in the first place.

Sometimes healing looks like this.
You still feel the trigger, but it no longer overtakes you.
You still notice the fear, but it no longer steals your voice.
You still remember what happened, but you no longer relive it.

The Holy Work of Reparenting

This is what I learned. Triggers are information.

They are not proof that you are broken.
They are proof that you are human.

A trigger is the body saying, "This feels familiar. We have been here before, and I want to protect you."

Healing happens when we stop fighting the signal and start listening to it, without allowing it to control us.

Learning from a trigger does not mean obeying it. It means understanding it.

This is not spiritual weakness.
It is emotional wisdom.

The Trigger Is Not the Teacher. The Wound Is.

A trigger is not the problem. It is the pointer.

It flashes and says there is an unhealed place here.
It reveals a lie that is still trying to live.

When I finally saw it this way, something inside me softened.

I stopped asking myself why I was still like this.
Why I was still reacting.
What was wrong with me.

I realized the triggered version of me was not my enemy.
She was my younger self, still asking to be protected.

She was the girl who learned to brace.
The woman who learned to stay alert.
The person who learned how to survive.

Now healing means I become a safe place for her.

I speak to myself the way God speaks to me, with patience, truth, and compassion.

This chapter is not about erasing triggers.
It is about learning what to do when they arrive.

Trauma may have introduced the trigger, but it does not get to write the ending.

I am learning that I can be triggered and still be wise.
I can feel activated and still choose peace.
I can feel fear and still walk forward.

Triggers are not the authority over my life.

God is restoring me in my reactions, in my nervous system, and in the parts of me that still flinch.

And that means the trauma does not win.

REFLECTION

Name It, Release It, Replace It

Name it.
What moments cause my body to tense, my thoughts to race, or my heart to shut down?

Release it.
What quiet lie is this trigger trying to confirm or resurrect within me?

Replace it.
What steady, grounding truth does God want to root me in when I feel emotionally activated?

Truth to repeat.
This is a trigger, not a prophecy over my life.

JOURNALING PROMPTS

1. My body reacts most often when I feel dismissed, rushed, unsafe, or unseen.

2. The feeling beneath my trigger is usually fear, grief, loneliness, or a longing to be protected.

3. This trigger reminds me of moments when I did not have the tools, voice, or strength to defend myself.

4. The lie it tries to prove is that I am not safe, not valued, or destined to relive the same pain.

5. The truth I will speak instead is that God is present with me now, I am held, and I am not powerless.

6. My pause plan, what I will do next time, is to stop, breathe slowly, place my feet firmly on the ground, and speak truth before I respond.

DECLARATION

TRIGGERS ARE NOT MY LEADER

I am not ruled by trauma responses that were formed in seasons of survival.
I am not governed by fear that no longer has authority over me.
I am not controlled by the past that God is actively redeeming.

I can pause even when my instincts want to react.
I can breathe through discomfort without fleeing or fighting.
I can choose a response aligned with wisdom and peace.

This is a trigger, not the truth about who I am.
This is an echo of an old wound, not a prophecy of my future.
This is a memory passing through my body, not my identity.

God is healing me at the root, not just the surface.
And I am safe to soften, safe to rest, and safe to heal.

BREATH PRAYER

Inhale. God, I am safe now.
Exhale. I return to this present moment.

Inhale. This is only an echo.
Exhale. It is not my reality.

Inhale. You are close to me.
Exhale. My body can calm.

Inhale. I choose peace over panic.
Exhale. I respond with wisdom and clarity.

CLOSING PRAYER

Father, in the name of Jesus, I surrender my nervous
system to Your peace.

Heal the places in me that still brace for impact.
Heal the parts of my body and mind that learned fear as a
form of wisdom.
Restore a deep sense of safety within me.

When triggers rise, help me slow down instead of
spiraling.
Help me name what is happening without shame or self
judgment.
Help me speak life and truth over my reactions.

Your Word says that You have not given me a spirit of fear, but power, love, and a sound mind, as written in 2 Timothy 1 verse 7.

So I receive power over panic.
I receive love over self protection.
I receive a sound, steady mind over trauma loops.

I am not controlled by what was.
I am led by Your Spirit who is present now.
And I am healing completely, deeply, and gently.

In Jesus' name, Amen.

Chapter Eleven

THE REINTRODUCTION

KEY SCRIPTURES

"If anyone is in Christ, they are a new creation."
2 Corinthians 5:17

"He has sent me to bind up the brokenhearted."
Isaiah 61:1

"To give them beauty for ashes." Isaiah 61:3

"He who began a good work in you will carry it on to completion." Philippians 1:6

WHAT THIS CHAPTER HOLDS

Reintroduction means you were present before, but not fully visible.

Not because you were absent,
but because you were armored.

This chapter is not about becoming someone new.
It is about coming home to who you have always been
beneath the protection, beneath the performance, beneath
the roles you learned to play in order to survive.

This is the return of the real you.
Not a stranger.
Not a curated version.

Just you.
Healed enough to stand.
Honest enough to stay.

INTERLUDE

YOU DO NOT OWE AN EXPLANATION TOUR

Healing changes the way you show up in the world.

And when you show up changed, people notice.
Some will ask questions with curiosity.
Some will ask questions with resistance.
Some will project confusion, discomfort, or
disappointment.

But you do not owe everyone a detailed narrative of your
becoming.

You are allowed to arrive as you are now.
Without footnotes.
Without disclaimers.
Without permission.

THE RETURN OF YOU

Reintroduction implies that something familiar has been absent.
Not lost.
Not erased.
Just unseen.

This is not the debut of a stranger.
It is the return of you.

After the walls have been identified.
After the pain has been named.
After the false identities have loosened their grip.
There comes a quiet moment when you stand face to face with yourself and realize that you did not actually know yourself as well as you thought.

Healing changes how you occupy your own body, your own thoughts, your own life.
And once that change takes root, life requires an introduction.

MEETING YOURSELF WITHOUT THE ARMOR

For a long time, armor felt like identity.

Strength replaced softness.
Independence replaced connection.
Control replaced trust.

These were not flaws. They were strategies.
They kept you moving when stopping felt too dangerous.
They kept you functioning when feeling would have overwhelmed you.

But armor is heavy.

When healing begins to remove it, you feel exposed.
Not weak, but unfamiliar.

You move differently now.
You respond differently.
You notice that the reflexes that once defined you no longer lead.

This is where the reintroduction begins.
You meet yourself without constant readiness for impact.
Without anticipating loss at every turn.
Without the pressure to prove that you survived.

And it feels disorienting, because peace does not demand performance.

RETURNING TO SPACES THAT REMEMBER THE OLD YOU

One of the most difficult aspects of healing is reentering environments that only recognize your former self.

People remember the version of you who was guarded.
Who was silent.
Who over gave or withdrew.
Who complied in order to keep the peace.

They may not immediately recognize who you are becoming.

And that is okay.

Growth does not require consensus.
The reintroduction is not an explanation tour.

You do not owe justification for your boundaries.
You do not owe defense for your voice.
You do not owe permission slips for your change.

You are allowed to arrive as you are now, even if it disturbs expectations.
Healing rewrites how you occupy space.

LEARNING TO RESPOND INSTEAD OF REACT

The healed version of you pauses.

Where there was once immediacy, there is now
discernment.
Where there was once defensiveness, there is now
choice.

At first, this feels unnatural.

Triggers still exist, but they no longer decide the ending.
You notice the urge to retreat, to lash out, to shut down.
And instead of obeying it, you ask what this moment
actually requires.

This is not restraint.
This is self trust.

The reintroduction includes learning how to move at the
pace of wisdom instead of fear.

REDEFINING RELATIONSHIPS

As you change, relationships adjust.
Some expand.
Some strain.
Some quietly dissolve.

Certain connections deepen because they were rooted in
truth.

Others struggle because they depended on who you used to be.

This can bring grief, even when the change is healthy.

Healing clarifies compatibility.
You stop forcing alignment.
You stop overextending to preserve closeness.
You stop confusing history with destiny.

The reintroduction teaches you that connection should never cost you yourself.

BECOMING VISIBLE AGAIN

There was a season when hiding felt necessary.

Visibility invited judgment.
Expression invited correction.
Authenticity felt unsafe.

So you learned how to disappear just enough to survive.

Healing restores your voice.

You begin speaking without apology.
Taking up space without shrinking.
Allowing your presence to be felt instead of minimized.

Being seen no longer feels like danger.
It feels like honesty.

This is one of the bravest moments of the reintroduction.
Allowing yourself to be known as you are now, not as
you were then.

LIVING WITHOUT CONSTANT SELF INTERROGATION

Unhealed pain questions everything.
Did I say too much.
Did I do enough.
Was that wrong.

Healing quiets that internal interrogation.

You begin trusting your intentions.
Believing your discernment.
Resting in the truth that perfection is not the price of
worthiness.

The reintroduction includes learning how to live without
monitoring yourself for mistakes.

Peace replaces hypervigilance.

REENTERING PURPOSE WITH CLARITY

Purpose feels different after healing.

It is no longer driven by proving, fixing, or
compensating.
It is rooted in alignment.

You choose what you pursue not from obligation, but resonance.
You recognize what fits and what does not.

The reintroduction into purpose is gentle.
It is intentional.
It is free from urgency.

You no longer chase meaning.
You respond to it.

And what is meant for you meets you without force.

ALLOWING JOY TO STAY

Joy used to feel temporary.

You enjoyed cautiously, bracing for interruption.
Preparing for the drop that always seemed to follow the high.

Healing disrupts that expectation.

You begin letting joy linger.
Not because life is perfect, but because pain no longer dictates the forecast.

You stop apologizing for happiness.
Stop minimizing good moments.
Stop preparing for loss before it arrives.

Joy becomes something you host, not something you manage.

INTRODUCING YOURSELF TO THE FUTURE

The reintroduction is not only to people.
It is to possibility.

You begin imagining a future not shaped by fear of
repetition.
You consider paths you once dismissed.
You allow yourself to want without immediately
calculating the cost.

Hope feels reasonable again.
Not naive.
Not reckless.
Just honest.

You introduce yourself to the idea that life can be
expansive, not merely manageable.

INTEGRATION, NOT PERFECTION

Healing does not erase complexity.

You still have memories.
You still hesitate at times.
You still hear the old instincts whisper.

But they no longer lead.

Integration means honoring where you have been
without living there.
You carry your story with wisdom, not weight.

THE COURAGE TO STAY PRESENT

Perhaps the greatest mark of healing is presence.

You are no longer bracing for the next impact or
replaying the last one.
You inhabit moments fully.
You listen without defensiveness.
You engage without armor.

The reintroduction anchors you in now.

And in this space, you realize something quietly
powerful.
You are not returning to life.
You are arriving fully awake.

SAYING HELLO TO YOURSELF

This chapter does not end with fanfare.
It ends with recognition.

You look at your life, your posture, your choices, and
you see yourself clearly.

Not fragmented.
Not hidden.
Not hardened.

Just whole.

The reintroduction is complete when you no longer feel
compelled to explain who you are.
You simply live as her.

Present.
Grounded.
Becoming.

And this time, you stay.

REFLECTION

Name It, Release It, Replace It

Name it
What version of me did I live as to survive?

Release it
Where am I still wearing armor out of habit?

Replace it
What does arriving as her look like in daily life?

Truth to repeat
I do not owe an explanation tour for my healing.

JOURNALING PROMPTS

1. The old version of me was known for

   _____________.

2. The healed version of me is learning

   _____________.

3. A boundary I am no longer explaining is

   _____________.

4. A relationship shifting in this season is

   _____________.

5. I am allowing joy to stay by _____________.

DECLARATION

I ARRIVE AS HER

I arrive as her.
Not fragmented.
Not hidden.
Not hardened.

I arrive with voice.
I arrive with peace.

I do not apologize for my becoming.
I do not shrink to preserve comfort.

I live as her.
And I stay.

BREATH PRAYER

Inhale: God, I am present.

Exhale: I release performance.

Inhale: I can be seen.

Exhale: I do not have to hide.

CLOSING DECLARATION

I am not returning to life.
I am arriving.

Whole enough to be honest.
Healed enough to stay.
Free enough to be seen.

My name is not what I survived.
My name is held in God.

MY NAME IS NOT…DECLARATIONS

DECLARATIONS: "MY NAME IS NOT"

My name is not the pain I survived.
My name is not the wounds left by another's choices.

My name is not molestation.
My name is not loss.
My name is not the season that broke me open and left me questioning my worth.
My name is not barren, empty, or forgotten.
My name is not rejection, abandonment, or shame.

My name is written in His promise, etched by grace and sealed by truth.
I am chosen on purpose, not by accident.
I am deeply loved, without condition or hesitation.
I am whole, even where I am still healing.
I am seen completely and hidden safely in God.
I am becoming who Heaven has always known me to be.

DECLARATIONS: "I BREAK AGREEMENT"

Today, with clarity and courage, I break agreement with shame that cloaks itself in humility.
I break agreement with fear that pretends to be wisdom.
I break agreement with numbness that imitates peace but steals my joy.
I break agreement with survival that tried to become my identity instead of my testimony.

I cancel every false word I accepted in silence when my
voice felt too small to fight back.
I refuse to partner with condemnation, accusation, or self
hatred.
I choose alignment with Heaven's truth.
I answer to God's voice alone, the voice that restores,
affirms, and calls me forward.

DECLARATIONS: "I AM FRUITFUL"

I am fruitful in ways that endure beyond sight and
seasons.
My life multiplies wisdom, love, healing, compassion,
and faith wherever I am planted.
I carry legacy not through comparison, but through lives
touched and hearts changed.
I will not dishonor my fruit simply because it looks
different than I once imagined.

God's blessing is not one dimensional or confined to a
single outcome.
God's goodness over my life is expansive, intentional,
and enough.
I am faithful with what I have been given, and God
Himself calls that fruitful.

DECLARATIONS: "I LAY IT DOWN"

I lay down burdens that were never mine to carry.
I lay down false responsibility and misplaced guilt.

I release the weight of outcomes I could not control.
I lay down the need to be needed and the habit of bracing
for disappointment.

I receive rest without guilt or explanation.
I receive peace without apology, knowing I am held,
covered, and safe.

GUIDED JOURNAL

GUIDED JOURNAL: "NAME IT"

Write without censoring. Finish each sentence.

1. The burden I carried that was never mine was
___________.

2. Letting go felt unsafe because ___________.

3. I answered to the name ___________ for too long.

4. Shame tried to convince me ___________.

5. The tears I held back were connected to ___________.

6. Memory tries to define me when ___________.

7. My wall was built because ___________.

8. I am ready to grow beyond ___________.

9. My potential is hidden under ___________.

10. I am reintroducing myself as ___________.

GUIDED JOURNAL: "RELEASE IT"

Write your answers as a release prayer.

• I release the belief that ___________.

• I release the fear of ___________.

• I release the habit of ___________.

• I release the need to prove ___________.

• I release the label __________.

• I release the memory that keeps replaying __________.

• I release the wall I built around __________.

What I am laying down today:

____

GUIDED JOURNAL: "REPLACE IT"

Now write what truth will replace it.

• God calls me __________.

• I am learning to trust by __________.

• The truth I will repeat is ___________.

• The healed version of me responds by ___________.

Use This Page When You Do Not Know What to Pray

Return to these pages as resting places for your heart. Each chapter is an invitation to meet God honestly wherever you are, without striving or performance.

1. When you are laying your burdens down, turn to Chapter 1 Prayer.

2. When surrender feels unsafe and vulnerability is difficult, return to Chapter 2 Affirmation.

3. When false names or old labels try to return, anchor yourself in Chapter 3 Prayer.

4. When shame attempts to measure your worth, be held by Chapter 4 Prayer.

5. When you cannot access your tears or emotions feel out of reach, rest in Chapter 5 Prayer.

6. When memory feels heavy and the past presses close, linger with Chapter 6 Closing Reflection.

7. When you are ready to expand again and breathe more freely, step into Chapter 7 Closing Reflection.

8. When the wall rises before your words do, declare truth through Chapter 8 Brick by Brick Declaration.

9. When you are stepping fully into purpose, stand firm with Chapter 9 Closing Declaration.

10. When you are arriving as the healed version of yourself, speak life with Chapter 10 I Arrive As Her Declaration.

In Case You Need a Starting Prayer

Father,

Thank you for restoring what I did not know how to repair. Thank You for meeting me exactly where I am and gently leading me toward freedom. Thank You for never rushing my healing and never turning away from my wounds.

Today, I renounce every lie that tried to define me, every borrowed name I accepted out of fear, and every voice that told me I had to earn love through survival. I release the burdens I carried alone, the weight I mistook for strength, and the exhaustion I learned to call normal.

I receive Your truth, the truth that brings clarity, peace, and wholeness. I receive the identity You spoke over me before I ever doubted myself. Teach me to trust You in the quiet spaces where nothing is explained but everything is held.

Heal me carefully and with intention. Strengthen me gently, without pressure or force. Restore my heart in ways that feel safe and lasting.

And let my life reflect the person You always knew I was becoming.

In Jesus' name, Amen.

THE TESTIMONY

This book stands as living proof of what God can
restore.
It is evidence that what was broken was not discarded,
that what was lost was not forgotten,
and that even the deepest wounds can become holy
ground.

Thank You, God, for:

• Remaining near in every season of my life,
in the loud moments of joy and in the quiet stretches
where You felt distant,
yet never absent.

• Grace, unearned and unending,
for lifting me when my legs could no longer carry me,
and holding me when surrender was all I had left.

• Faith, not just in what You can do,
but in who You are: steady, faithful, and true,
even when my understanding fell short.

• The version of me who survived,
the one who endured unseen battles and kept breathing
through the pain.
I see you now. I honor you.

• The version of me who is becoming,
the one learning to trust again, to hope again, to rise with

wisdom instead of fear.
I will guard you fiercely.

To every soul who has carried pain in silence,
who has learned to smile while breaking inside,
may these pages remind you that you were never alone,
and that your suffering did not define you.
You are not what you endured.
You are what God is still restoring.